REA FRIEND OF ACPL

Y0-AKX-943

A spiritual almanac

Don Jennings
Rom. 8:28

**DO NOT REMOVE
CARDS FROM POCKET**

3-3-97

**ALLEN COUNTY PUBLIC LIBRARY
FORT WAYNE, INDIANA 46802**

You may return this book to any agency, branch,
or bookmobile of the Allen County Public Library.

DEMCO

STEEPLE BOOKS

This series offers the concerned reader basic guidelines and *practical* applications of religion for today's world. Although decidedly Christian in focus and emphasis, the series embraces all denominations and modes of Bible-based belief relevant to our lives today. All volumes in the Steeple series are originals, freshly written to provide a fresh perspective on current—and yet timeless—human dilemmas. This is a series for our times. Among the books:

How to Read the Bible
James Fischer

How to Live Your Faith
L. Perry Wilbur

A Spiritual Handbook for Women
Dandi Daley Knorr

Temptation: How Christians Can Deal with It
Frances Carroll

With God on Your Side: A Guide to Finding Self-Worth Through Total Faith
Doug Manning

A Daily Key for Today's Christians: 365 Key Texts of the New Testament
William E. Bowles

Walking in the Garden: Inner Peace from the Flowers of God
Paula Connor

How to Bring Up Children in the Catholic Faith
Carol and David Powell

*Sex in the Bible:
An Introduction to What the Scriptures Teach Us About Sexuality*
Michael R. Cosby

*How to Talk with God Every Day of the Year:
A Book of Devotions for Twelve Positive Months*
Frances Hunter

*God's Conditions for Prosperity:
How to Earn the Rewards of Christian Living*
Charles Hunter

Pilgrimages: A Guide to the Holy Places of Europe for Today's Traveler
Paul Lambourne Higgins

*Journey into the Light: Lessons of Pain and Joy
to Renew Your Energy and Strengthen Your Faith*
Dorris Blough Murdock

DON JENNINGS

A Spiritual Almanac

Guidelines for Better Living
Each Month of the Year

A SPECTRUM BOOK

Prentice-Hall, Inc., Englewood Cliffs, New Jersey 07632

Library of Congress Cataloging in Publication Data

Jennings, Don.
  A spiritual almanac.

  (Steeple books)
  "A Spectrum Book."
  Includes index.
  1. Devotional calendars.   I. Title.   II. Series.
BV4811.J4 1984   242   84-6963
ISBN 0-13-834755-7
ISBN 0-13-834748-4 (pbk.)

Allen County Public Library
900 Webster Street
PO Box 2270
Fort Wayne, IN 46801-2270

© 1984 by Prentice-Hall, Inc., Englewood Cliffs, New Jersey 07632.
All rights reserved. No part of this book may be reproduced in any form
or by any means without permission in writing from the publisher.
A Spectrum Book. Printed in the United States of America.

1 2 3 4 5 6 7 8 9 10

ISBN 0-13-834755-7
ISBN 0-13-834748-4 {PBK.}

Editorial/production supervision
and book design: Joe O'Donnell Jr.
Cover design: Mike Freeland
Manufacturing buyer: Frank Grieco

This book is available at a special discount when ordered in
bulk quantities. Contact Prentice-Hall, Inc., General
Publishing Division, Special Sales, Englewood Cliffs, N.J. 07632.

Prentice-Hall International, Inc., *London*
Prentice-Hall of Australia Pty. Limited, *Sydney*
Prentice-Hall Canada Inc., *Toronto*
Prentice-Hall of India Private Limited, *New Delhi*
Prentice-Hall of Japan, Inc., *Tokyo*
Prentice-Hall of Southeast Asia Pte. Ltd., *Singapore*
Whitehall Books Limited, *Wellington, New Zealand*
Editora Prentice-Hall do Brasil Ltda., *Rio de Janeiro*

Contents

Preface/vii

JANUARY
FACING NEW OPPORTUNITIES/1

FEBRUARY
THE CHALLENGE OF OUR HERITAGE/16

MARCH
LIFE'S CONCERNS/29

APRIL
THE HOPE OF THINGS ETERNAL/40

MAY
THE HOME AND FAMILY/52

JUNE
YOUTH AND THE FUTURE/72

JULY
FREEDOM'S COST/87

AUGUST
KEYS TO SUCCESSFUL LIVING/99

SEPTEMBER
HOW TO FIND PEACE/112

OCTOBER
INFLUENCING OTHERS/125

NOVEMBER
COUNTING OUR BLESSINGS/137

DECEMBER
TAKING THE ROAD TO BETHLEHEM/152

Index/165

Preface

It was almost midnight as I left the hospital. I had tarried long after my regular hour of departure to stand by a young father and mother whose young son was not expected to live through the night.

As I waited at an intersection for the traffic light to change, I noted on a well-lit church bulletin board the words "If your day is hemmed with prayer, it is less likely to unravel."

Keeping life from going stale or unraveling is the aim and longing of most of us, and that is what this book is all about. I earnestly hope the reader will discover in the following pages some guidelines for better living—and I pray that the thoughts presented herein may be an inspiration to all who come across them.

ACKNOWLEDGEMENTS

The poem on page 46, "There Is No Death," is by John L. McCreery.

The hymn on page 41 is excerpted from "Sunrise," by W. C. Poole, and appears courtesy of the Rodeheaver, Hall-Mack Co.

The verses on pages 43 and 50 are excerpts from "Christ Arose," by

Robert Lowery, and it appears by permission of Rodeheaver, Hall-Mack Co.

The excerpts from "Wonderful Peace," by W. D. Cornell, page 45; "God Will Take Care of You," by C. D. Martin, page 92; "Trust and Obey," by John Sammis, page 104; "Just as I Am," by Charlotte Elliott, page 129; "My Father's World," by Maltbie Babcock, page 141; "Our Best," by C. S. Kirk, page 142; "All the Way My Savior Leads Me," by Fanny Crosby, page 151; and from "My Prayer," pages 126 and 127, are included by permission of Charles Scribner's Sons, New York, New York.

The lyric appearing on page 52 is from "Bless This House," music by May H. Brahe and words by Helen Taylor. It is printed here by permission of Boosey & Hawkes, Inc., © copyright 1927, 1932 by Boosey & Co., Ltd., renewed 1954, 1959.

The poem on pages 52 and 53 are extracts from "Home," by Edgar A. Guest. It is reprinted from *Collected Verse of Edgar A. Guest,* © copyright 1934 by Contemporary Books, Inc., Chicago, Illinois. Used by permission.

The verses on pages 59 and 60 are extracts from a hymn by Virgil and Blanche Brock. It is reprinted with permission from Rodeheaver, Hall-Mack Co, Winona Lake, Indiana.

The verse on page 89 is from a poem by Josiah Holland. It is used by permission of Chares Scribner's Sons, New York, New York.

A brief account of Horsto Spafford and "It Is Well With My Soul," page 100, are from *Hymn Stories for Programs,* by Ernest K. Emurian, copyright 1963 by Baker Book House and used by permission.

The excerpts from "Columbus" that appear on page 105 are by Joaquin Miller. They are reprinted by permission of Charles Scribner's Sons, 597 5th Avenue, New York, New York.

The verse on page 158 is from "How Great Thou Art," by Stuart K. Hine. © Copyright 1953, 1955, renewed 1981 by Manna Music, Inc., 2111 Kenmere Avenue, Burbank, California 91504. International copyright secured. All rights reserved. Used by permission.

Throughout the book, excerpts have been used from the author's "Sermonettes" column, published by the *American Agriculturist* for the past six years. These are reprinted courtesy of the American Agriculturist, Inc.

A Spiritual Almanac

Within the pages of this book,
you will find an inspirational series of *thoughts*
for each month of the year. It is my hope that
the wisdom and compassion the reader finds here
as he journeys through the year
will help him to live life at its best.

JANUARY

Facing New Opportunities

BEGINNING AGAIN

"Ring out the old, Ring in the new." So begins a poem for the new year written by Alfred Tennyson, a well-known English poet. Time marches on, and the years come and go. When we think of this season of the year, we pause to meditate upon what has been and what we hope will be.

For many years I have enjoyed a beautiful dahlia in my flower garden. Each year it has produced the largest blossoms of any dahlia plant we have ever had. Each fall, as the frost has wilted the dahlia, I have dug up the clump of bulbs and stored them away. Then in the spring I have replanted those bulbs and tried to produce larger blossoms than the year before.

The new year is like our prize dahlia. We hope and pray that each year will be better than the one before. It is a new start, but not without the memories and experiences of the past. As we begin this season, we pray that we might profit by our past mistakes as well as our past accomplishments.

The Psalm-writer expressed the prayer of many of us when he said, "So teach us to number our days, that we may apply our hearts unto wisdom" (Psalm 90:12). He urged us to make each day count with the wisdom that belongs to all who ask for it. We are not to boast of what we shall do in the year ahead but to keep ourselves available, ". . . for thou knowest not what a day may bring forth" (Proverbs 27:1).

We should not approach the new year with fear, but with faith. As a youngster on the farm, there were times when I feared the last minutes of the old year. I was worried that the end of the year might bring the end of the world. As an adult, with my life fully committed to the Creator, Who holds the future in His hands as He hath the past and the present, I look to each new year with hope and faith. I do not know what the future holds, but I do know Who holds the future.

Frances Havergal, the English poet, expressed our prayer for the new year when she wrote:

Another year is dawning.
Dear Master, let it be
In working or in waiting,
Another year for Thee.
Another year of service,
Of witness for Thy love,
Another year of training
For holier work above.

TOMORROW BEGINS TODAY

Tomorrow begins today! The future is now! To a great extent the fruits of the new year will depend on how we care for our vineyard today.

There are those who see only their yesterdays. Someone long ago observed that those who live in the past wake up to find that they have dissipated the present. It is good to look back in memory, but it is better to look forward with hope. Remembering past victories encourages us for tomorrow's challenges. Recalling the failures of the past helps us to make wise decisions in the future.

A young boy who was away at camp wrote to his parents at home. In the letter he said, "We went on a hike yesterday. It was a mountain trip. It was fun—except we found that we had climbed the wrong mountain!"

Gaining a right perspective of the future helps us to guard against climbing the wrong mountain.

Tomorrow begins today. Someone once suggested that we should plan this day as though it were the first day of the rest of our lives and live it as though it might be the last.

The Psalm-writer gave us words of wisdom when he wrote, "So teach us to number our days, that we may apply our hearts unto wisdom" (Psalm 90:12). The application of wisdom is a desperate need of our time. We need a double portion as we enter another year. The disappointments of the past must not dim the hopes of the future. We may not know what the future holds for us, but we do know Who holds the future.

John relates a part of the revelation that came to him while he was on the Isle of Patmos: "... behold, I have set before thee an open door, and no man can shut it ..." (Revelation 3:8). Only we ourselves can ignore the open door of opportunity and obligation that is before us.

The world hungers for those who still have faith in the present and hope for the future. Especially, there is need for those who have faith in God, Who is the same yesterday and today, and forever. It can truly be a happy new year if we keep that faith and, more, put it into practice.

LOOKING AHEAD

The frost arrived before we were prepared for it. My neighbor hurried outside to gather the seed from his favorite flowers to plant again in the following May. Watching my good friend from my side of the fence as he prepared for the future, I smiled and called out, "Uncle Orlo, you are always looking ahead."

What better words can be said of anyone? Here was a neighbor who had enjoyed the past . . . lived in the present . . . and prepared for the future.

We have seen many harvests come and go. Whether we shall see another new one, only God knows. But we must save some seeds from the past if we are to be ready for the future. This is true not only of material things but of the spiritual as well. As Uncle Orlo once observed, "We should work as though we will live forever but live as though we might die tonight."

As I look ahead into the coming year, I do so with anticipation. I have reached some goals during this past year. Other hopes and plans have not yet materialized. But, God willing, I shall keep striving. I once heard Gabriel Heatter, a radio commentator, say, "Life begins when a man fixes a goal for himself. It ends when there is no goal ahead."

The author of the Epistle to the Hebrews was a person who was always looking ahead with faith and hope. He entreated his listeners to remember the faith of those of the past. He also reminds us that we are to ". . . run with patience the race that is set before us, Looking unto Jesus the author and finisher of our faith . . ." (Hebrews 12:1-2).

In the last Bible my mother used before her eternal departure, I found a piece of paper on which she had written, "I know not what the future holds, but I know Who holds the future." It was the confidence she placed in her Lord that kept her faith alive each day of her life.

As we complete the living of another year, we pause to thank God for His bounteous blessings of the past. We look ahead and pray that the new year may be a year not only of material and physical well-being but a year when peace shall reign again in our troubled world—the kind of peace that comes when we submit our will to God's will.

FEELING THE PULL

Gravity was the law that said, we used to think, that everything that went up would come down. In these days of exploration into outer space, we have discovered that it means this—and more.

To escape from the earth's gravity, our astronauts flying to the moon traveled through space at a speed of twenty-four thousand miles per hour! After three days, they crossed an invisible boundary beyond which they were in the lunar sphere of influence. They found themselves in a new experience of gravity. We are told that they went from the pull of the earth's gravity to that of the moon's.

As I dwelt on this interesting aspect of life, I thought of how much it resembles the passing of time. We no sooner experience the journey through one year before we feel the gravity, or pull, of another. It seems that the more years one experiences, the more one stands in awe of God's plan for our universe of time and space. The Psalm-writer expressed our feelings when he wrote, "The heavens declare the glory of God; and the firmament showeth forth his handywork" (Psalm 19:1).

Is it any wonder that Jim Irvin, one of the astronauts, after his experience on the moon, was overwhelmed with the "holiness of the place" and returned to earth to engage in evangelical preaching?

The more we are drawn into another year, the farther we leave behind the years of the past. We do not forsake the loyalties and the goals of the past, but we feel the pull of new loyalties and the vision of new and greater goals.

We do not know what lies ahead of us, but we do know how true are the words of the wise man who said, "Hear, O my son, and receive my sayings; and the years of thy life shall be many" (Proverbs 4:10).

Grandpa, entering into his grandson's experience of kite-flying, was trying his best to watch the kite as it lifted high into the sky. But failing eyesight made it impossible for him to follow the distant object. He reached for the string and with the smile of a boy, exclaimed, "Son, I can't see it, but I can feel its pull!"

We may not be able to see the wonders and hopes of the new year, but by faith in the God Who can, we may reach out and feel the *pull* of the year ahead. James Russell Lowell expressed our faith when he wrote, "... behind the dim unknown, standeth God within the shadow, keeping watch above His own."

"HIS MASTER'S VOICE"

Years ago one of the trademarks of the Victor Phonograph Company was the picture of a Victorola phonograph with a horn. In front of this horn sits a white dog, alert and listening. Beneath the picture are the words, "His Master's Voice." The sound reproduction, according to the company, is so perfect that the dog recognizes his master's voice.

The world is confused. Great numbers of people are disillusioned. Many have chosen wrong goals. Many others have been brainwashed, only later realizing that they have been hooked and are prisoners. They have listened too, but they have heeded the wrong voices. These people need and have our concern and prayers. Many others are like the sheep of whom Jesus spoke in the story of the Good Shepherd: "... and the sheep follow him: for they know his voice" (John 10:4).

Today there are many voices trying to command our attention. The television commercials that bombard our homes are one example. We need wisdom and courage to sort out and decide which is really our "Master's Voice."

Back in Old Testament days lived the prophet Eli. At times it seemed that he was a weak prophet. But we cannot forget that he trained a future prophet by the name of Samuel, for whom a title might well have been, "Samuel, the man whom God could help." If we were choosing a text for this young man who became a great prophet, it could likely be, "Speak, Lord; for thy servant heareth" (I Samuel 3:10).

One must not only *hear* his Master's voice but *trust* it. One of the most difficult words to accept is *trust*. If it is the voice of the doctor, we must trust his medicine and advice. If it is the teacher, we must have confidence in his or her instruction. If it is the voice of the Good Shepherd, we must not only trust His Word—we must follow it.

Jesus warned His followers of those whom they should not trust: "And a stranger will they not follow, but will flee from him: for they know not the voice of strangers" (John 10:5).

There is a voice of our day—our Master's Voice. For our own good and for the good of those whom we love, we need to listen, trust, and follow.

PATIENCE

"The success or failure of a cook depends on how well he follows the recipe," so advised a competent and entertaining cook. In our presence, he prepared a highly tasty and satisfying meal by faithfully following his own proven recipes.

After watching our host and enjoying his cooking, I concluded that a fruitful and peaceful life also depends on certain ingredients. One of those ingredients is patience. Webster's dictionary defines patience as a quality of calm endurance. Thomas Carylyle, a British philosopher, wrote, "Patience strengthens the spirit, sweetens the temper, stifles anger, and tramples upon temptation."

Peter, the apostle, lived, learned, and experienced many of the ways of life. From his accumulated wisdom he gives us the formula, or ingredient, for a fruitful and victorious life. As a part of that wise counsel, he wrote, "And to knowledge temperance; and to temperance patience; and to patience godliness..." (II Peter 1:6).

James, the brother and servant of our Lord, begins his

Epistle by saying, "But let patience have her perfect work, that we may be perfect and entire, wanting nothing" (James 1:4). Patience is a state of mind desired by each of us and a quality that is never attained one hundred percent by any of us.

Recently someone asked me, "Where does patience end and indifference begin?" Patience does not mean indifference. Patience is the virtue that teaches us to work, trust, and *wait*. It was the Psalm-writer of long ago who said, "Rest in the Lord, and wait patiently for Him. . . (Psalm 37:7). One does not reach the realm of patience by praying, "Grant me patience, Lord, but hurry."

I have discovered in my own life that patience is not a bequest, but a conquest. It is not something that I may inherit from my parents. I must work for it, pray for it, and practice it.

Norma White's neighbors were having coffee with her one morning. One of them observed, "Norma is so easygoing. Nothing ever seems to ruffle her. And she's so patient with her family."

Norma smiled. "Girls, it hasn't always been that way. I used to blow up. Then I tried counting to ten, but still I would fly off and say things I was sorry for later. Finally I prayed, 'Lord, You have to help me. I confess that I can't do it alone.' I find now that even though I'm not a perfect example of patience, life is much easier."

None of us will ever be perfect in any field of endeavor, but our lives are certainly made more harmonious and richer when we include as an ingredient a sincere prayer to God—daily—for patience.

THE VALUE OF FRIENDS

"I practiced flattery; I never pretended to make friends," Napoleon claimed. And there on a rocky little island he fretted away the last years of his life in exile, alone, without the benefit of true friends.

Who can estimate the value of friends? A friend is someone who knows all about you but still loves you. True friends are worth far more than their weight in gold. I have observed that having money and friends is easy—but having no money and friends is an accomplishment!

As we read of the life of Jesus during His earthly ministry, we discover that while He had some enemies, He also had many friends. Jesus took His disciples into His confidence in the Upper Room on that final night before His death on the cross. He said to them, "Henceforth I call you not servants . . . but I have called you friends . . ." (John 15:15). One translation of these words reads, "I no longer call you slaves, for a master does not confide in his slaves, now you are my friends, proved by the fact that I have told you everything the Father has told me."

First of all, friends are interested in who we are and who we can become, not in what we have. A friend who has to be bought will not be worth what you have to pay. Jesus knew that His disciples were not perfect, but He knew also that they were willing. He knew what they could become.

Second, friends have a concern for one another's needs and hopes for the future. Jesus, the disciples' Friend and Master, was trying to prepare His followers for the future, when He would no longer be with them in person. It was not easy, for they were thinking of temporal matters, such as a kingdom on earth with Jesus as their king. Jesus was talking of matters eternal. His was not a kingdom of this world, but a Heavenly kingdom.

The thoughtfulness of friends also means, we have been taught, that a true friend will lay down his life for those whom he loves. This is the ultimate price that Jesus was willing to pay so that He might bring to those whom He loved the abundant life now and for eternity.

We may or may not be called upon to lay down our lives for Him, but it is certain that we are called upon each day to stand up for Him. Being a friend knows no limit.

EXCESS BAGGAGE

Most of us have a drawer, a box, a room—someplace—where we store things for which we have no more use. We hold on to these things with the thought that they might come in handy someday. Often they just clutter up the premises and become nothing more than excess baggage.

Once in preparing to make a trip, the advice given me by an experienced traveler was, "Take only the bare necessities. You will gather enough extra baggage before you get back home." This is good advice, whether for a trip or as we travel the highways of life.

Prejudice is sometimes a part of our excess baggage, encumbering our travels through life. Prejudice is often difficult to leave behind. It became a part of our lives long ago, and it is now most difficult to discard.

Someone asked Oliver Herford, an American humorist of another generation, his opinion of the English novelist, Arnold Bennett. "To tell you the truth," Herford answered, "something I wrote once in a critical way concerning Arnold Bennett so prejudiced me against the man that I could never bear to read a word he wrote." When we harbor prejudice in our journey through life, it narrows our vision due to preconceived decisions, and we miss much of the joy of living.

Hatred is another item of excess baggage. Hatred impairs our health, shortens our lives, and disfigures our personalities. An attitude of hatred blinds us to the values of compassion and forgiveness.

It was hatred that caused the brothers of Joseph to sell him to slave-traders while on their way to Egypt. It was forgiveness, compassion, and love that caused Joseph to return good for evil in his dealings with his brothers. The climax of the incident arrived when Joseph said to his repentant brothers, "... ye thought evil against me; but God meant it unto good, to bring to pass, as it is this day, to save much people alive" (Genesis 50:20).

In His Sermon on the Mount, Jesus said in part, "Ye hath heard that it hath been said, Thou shalt love thy neighbour, and hate thine enemy. But I say unto you, Love your enemies, bless them that curse you, and pray for them which despitefully use you, and persecute you . . ." (Matthew 5:43-44).

There are many things that may impair our journey through life, but there is one thing that is never excess baggage: Love. Leave prejudice and hatred behind, but be sure to take along a generous supply of love. God's love. It will lighten and enhance your journey—for love never fails.

HELPLESS, NOT HOPELESS

"I may be helpless, but I'm not hopeless," responded young Noel George with an infectious smile.

Weeks earlier I had been in the hospital emergency room when Noel was brought in. He had been in an accident on his father's farm and was paralyzed from his waist down. As days went by, Noel never gave up. He followed faithfully every direction of his therapist and his faith did not waver.

Noel has the kind of vibrant courage and personality that is contagious. He knew how close he had come to death, and he realized—after many frustrations—that he had a long way to go. I was expressing a word of encouragement that morning when he responded with those brave words.

What one of us has not experienced feelings of hopelessness, futility, and aloneness; times when future loomed uncertain before us? There were days when we were about as low as we could be. Fear had begun to paralyze us. Should we give up in despair? Then, with just a glimmer of faith and the encouragement of a good friend, we said, "I may be helpless, but I'm not hopeless."

Countless men and women, from the time of the Creation, have faced these periods of helplessness. But they did not give up. They too knew that they were helpless alone, but with God, they were not hopeless.

"What time I am afraid, I will trust in thee," David wrote in Psalm 56:3. He knew that his trust in the Lord would not be in vain. He had found that God would never leave him nor forsake him.

When our son Martel was eight years old, he had to have minor surgery for a bone condition. As we walked into the operating room and Martel was placed upon the table, he confided, "Daddy, if you will hold my hand, I won't be afraid." Needless to say, when Martel went to sleep, his daddy was holding his hand. Confidence displayed in the presence of helplessness encourages hope.

Zechariah, the prophet, endeavored to lead his people and to give them hope in the coming Messiah. In their time of deep despair, Zachariah implored them, "Turn you to the strong hold, ye prisoners of hope . . ." (Zechariah 9:12).

It is good to be a "prisoner of hope." Isaac Watts, English hymn-writer, was a "prisoner of hope." During the despair of the English people over the illness and death of "good Queen Anne," Isaac Watts wrote, O God our help in ages past, Our hope for years to come.

Henry F. Lyte, when weakened in body and knowing his days to be numbered, wrote his hymn of hope in the face of helplessness and included the words, "Help of the helpless, O abide with me."

If God be for us, who can be against us? With confidence, we too can say, "I may be helpless, but I'm not hopeless"—for our hope rests in our God.

SOMETHING EXTRA

"Whatever happened to that extra lump of brown sugar the grocery-keeper used to give us when we went with Mother to do the trading?" I reminisced to an old friend recently.

Uncle Charley White was that kind of storekeeper. Like

many others of his day, he believed that nothing was lost by giving more than his customers were paying for. Today we would call it public relations—something extra, like the frosting on the cake or the rebate when you purchase a new car.

Down through the years I have known many who have done more than they were asked to do. It is like giving service with a smile. Jesus called it going the second mile.

In His Sermon on the Mount, Jesus was talking about doing more than we are obligated to do: "And whosoever shall compel thee to go a mile, go with him twain" (Matthew 5:41). As was the custom in those days, and even a law, a soldier passing through the village could compel a citizen to carry his personal equipment for the distance of one mile. Jesus was saying that we were to go the second mile, beyond our obligation.

The real joy in life comes when we go beyond that which is expected of us. It is like the extra half-dozen apples my father used to place on top of the basket when it was already full. It not only pleased the customer but gave much satisfaction to my father.

Last fall Mrs. Jennings and I were on our way from Nashville to Knoxville, Tennessee, when a tire on our car blew out. A man who had been driving behind us stopped to help. Mrs. Jennings was so impressed by the Good Samaritan act of this young man that she was inspired to say, "You must be a real Christian."

Our new friend smiled and responded with, "No, I am not a Christian. I am a Jew."

This man was going the second mile. He was doing something that he was not at all obligated to do. Both Thelma and I thought that it was truly a splendid deed.

When we go beyond the call of duty in any avenue of life, we are going the second mile. The rewards of doing something extra are many; but principally, in so doing, we are following the example of Jesus Himself.

A NEW LEAF

He came to my desk with quivering lip,
The lesson was done.
"Dear Teacher, I want a new leaf," he said,
"I have spoiled this one."

The above words are part of a poem that for many years has meant much to me. The author is anonymous, but the thought touches each of us, especially at this season of the year. The poet goes on to say:

In place of the leaf so strained and blotted,
I gave him a new one all unspotted
And into his sad eyes smiled,
"Do better now, my child."

Most of us come to the end of the year feeling that we have made many mistakes. We have tried. We have erased and tried again. But we must not despair. As a teacher of mine said long ago, "We have erasers on our pencils to correct our mistakes." Although we often say that we profit by the mistakes of the past, we feel better when we can encouraged by the hopes of the future.

The remainder of the New Leaf poem says;

I went to the throne with quivering soul,
The old year was doen.
"Dear Father, hast Thou a new leaf for me? I have spoiled
*   this one."*
He took the old leaf, stained and blotted
And gave me a new one all unspotted.
And into my sad heart smiled, "Do better now, my child."

Each new day or new year presents us with another opportunity to do better that we have done in the past. It is an open door that no one can close. Peter, one of the disciples of Jesus, was a wave before he became a rock. The big fisherman was for a while only poor, blundering Peter. But Jesus saw many good qualities iin him and prayed for him. Time after time Jesus gave Peter a "new leaf," and Peter finally became the kind of disciple that Jesus needed and that Peter himself wanted to be.

Another year is before us. No one knows but God Himself what it has in store for us. There is one thing certain though—opportunities are ahead, not only opportunities to do better but to enlarge on the good that we accomplished in the past.

A new leaf has been given us, bearing the promise of God's Presence with the words, "Do better now, My child."

FEBRUARY

The Challenge of Our Heritage

FRUITS FROM ROOTS

Recently, I had the opportunity to speak at the Coles County Soil Conversation Stewardship annual meeting in Mattoon, Illinois. Our hosts, Mr. and Mrs. David Janas, graciously took us out to see some of the Lincoln countyside.

There at the Shiloh church cemetery, we paused at the graves of Thomas Lincoln and Sarah Bush Lincoln, father and stepmother of Abraham Lincoln. On the memorial stone I read the following: "Their humble but worthy home gave to the world Abraham Lincoln." Little did those humble parents of long ago realize that one of the most beloved and respected presidents of the United States was to emerge from their roots.

The fruits that are ours today have come from the roots of the past. Great nations come from small beginnings. The Declaration of Independence was written, revised, and signed by fifty-six courageous men. In it was the call to freedom, but by itself it was only the Declaration, only the paper. Our country had to undergo much sacrifice of blood, sweat, and tears—combined with continuous prayer—that we might enjoy the freedom of this day.

Carl Sandburg, poet, author, and historian, once observed, "We had better not forget from whence we have come and by whom." I might add that if we would keep our freedom, we would do well to not only remember from whence we have come but to keep the God-inspired hope that lies in the future ever before us. Though our fruits come from the faith of those of the past, we must be ever mindful of our place in the world's future.

When the Israelites crossed the Jordan River into the Promised Land of Canaan, Joshua had them set up twelve stones taken from the Jordan "That this may be a sign among you, that when your children ask their fathers in time to come saying, What mean ye by these stones? Then ye shall answer them, That the waters of Jordan were cut off before the ark of the covenant of the Lord; when it passed over Jordan ... these stones shall be a memorial unto the children of Israel forever" (Joshua 4:6-7).

As we pause again at the anniversary of the signing of the Declaration of Independence, let us also pause in gratitude for our roots from out of the past and thank God for those who trusted in His wisdom.

We today are the roots through which our children will reap the fruits of the future. May we keep before us a solemn vow of commitment to the God of yesterday, today, and forever.

A LIVING MEMORIAL

"That we here highly resolve that these dead shall not have died in vain...." Thus spoke President Abraham Lincoln on Thursday, November 19, 1863. His address at Gettysburg, Pennsylvania, dedicating a national cemetery for the dead of the

Civil War, lasted for only about five minutes. It is not remembered for its bravity but for its content. It was not only a memorial to the dead, it was a challenge to the living.

There have been millions of casualties as the result of the wars in which America has been involved. Those casulties have claimed many of the finest youth of the land. Each one hoped to live out his time on earth in peace and in the pursuit of happiness.

As we come again to the days we have set apart in their memory, the words of Lincoln not only reach our ears but into our hearts: ". . . that these dead shall not have died in vain."

If they have not died in vain, it will be because we endeavor, by God's help, to work for the peaceful settlement of our differences with other nations of the world. The price of peaceful settlement calls upon us for humility as well as for intellectual and compassionate wisdom. This is not a sign of weakness; it is a mark of strength.

If those young men have not died in vain, it will be because we who are survivors, and we who have experienced the horrors of war, bow our heads in memory of those whom we loved. At the same time, we lift our prayers to God, Whose mercy has spared us. And we pray, as we remember those of the past, that we shall be worthy of the hopeful and peaceful future.

The Psalm-writer spoke words of wisdom when he said, "Blessed is the nation whose God is the Lord . . ." (Psalm 33:12). Our nation has been blessed in many ways by the Great Creator. Many of those blessings we have dissipated. In so doing, we have disgraced those who have sacrificed for us.

On the other hand, we have shared in gratitude our rich blessings with those of the world who are less fortunate. It is in this expression of sharing that we revere the memory, of those courageous young men and women who gave their lives for us and our nation. It is in this kind of compassion that we find favor with God.

WE HAVE A HERITAGE

Thirty-three years before the Civil War, a young man of twenty-four and his bride left North Carolina. Their destination, like others of that part of the state, was Indiana.

This young couple could not sanction slavery. Their hope was for a better opportunity for their family and their neighbors. So poor were they that their only means of conveyance on the journey was a cart drawn by one horse.

One could best describe the life of this young couple during those early years as laden with privation, frugality, perseverance, determination—and blessed with a strong faith in God. That young man and his wife were my great-grandparents, Samuel and Margaret Madren Jennings.

Many of you have roots similar to mine. The privations of our forebears were severe, but their frugality and faith carried then through. Truly, we have a great heritage. Much of what we enjoy today—as a nation and as individuals—is ours because of the determination of those who have lived before us.

Abraham of Old Testament days, to whom we owe so much, left his home in Haran. "... he went out, not knowing whither he went" (Hebrews 11:8). Faith in God's promises kept him moving on. Because Abraham was faithful and kept striving toward his goal, others who followed after him were encouraged to do likewise.

The Faith Chapter (Hebrews 11) closes with the words, "God having provided some better thing for us, that they without us should not be made perfect." Generations are joined together like a chain, and each of us is a link. Those who led lives of faith depend on us to honor their legacy.

I have often asked myself, "what kind of a heritage am I leaving to my family and those whose lives I have touched? Will their lives be richer for my having lived? Have I tried, with

God's help, to carry on the ideals and hopes of those who have gone before me?"

Recently I received a letter from a young farmer who lost his father two years ago. He told me that he had inherited the farm and concluded his letter by saying: "I appreciate the inheritance of the farm, but I am most grateful for the memory of parents whose faith in God and life will continue to be a guiding light in my life."

Faith is not a bequest, but a conquest. We cannot bequeath our faith, but we can leave an example of faith in God. This can be our greatest gift to those who follow us.

I LOVE MY COUNTRY

I love my Country
Land of my birth
I love my Country
Grandest on earth.
Whene'er I hear those words so dear,
"God shed His grace on thee,"
I lift my voice in grateful praise: "America for me."

So goes the chorus of a song I composed for our bicentennial celebration in 1976.

Ralph Waldo Emerson, American philosopher and poet, once said, "America is another name for opportunity. Our whole history appears like a last effort of Divine Providence in behalf of the human race."

I love my Country for the opportunities it affords us. Not that opportunity is a finished product. Far from it. But it is a privilege to be able to invest my talents for a fruitful future. I recognize that I am to use these opportunities for the advantage of others, and in accepting these opportunities, I will accept certain responsibilities in behalf of God and man.

I love my Country for the privilege of freedom of speech. I may praise or criticize, but I must weigh my words so that I do not downgrade the Country that has lifted me up.

I love my Country for the privilege of freedom of worship. Our forefathers came to this land that they might not only find a place of material promise but that they might worship as they felt led.

In America I am free to worship or not to worship God by the dictates of my conscience. God grant that I may always enjoy the blessing of worshiping Him of Whom we sing: "Our Father's God to Thee, Author of liberty."

Last, but not least, I love my Country not because it is perfect but because as we discover our imperfections, we strive, by God's help, to correct them.

My song, to which I referred in the beginning, has another verse that goes like this:

'Tis not a perfect Land I know.
Our failures, faults abound,
But if our faith in God we show,
Our future's course is sound.

GOD'S MINORITIES

"One man with courage makes a majority," observed Andrew Jackson, seventh president of the United States and fearless military leader in the early years of our country's founding.

History, from the beginning of time, has often proven that some of our greatest men and women have not always been on the side of the majority. But how often the words, "One person and God make a majority," have turned out to be true. Some of our most famous inventors have seemed at times to be very much alone and have even been made fun of. But they won. This has been the case in many of the brave ventures undertaken for human and spiritual benefit.

During the time that Noah was building the ark, he was very much in the minority—but he won! When Gideon and his three hundred followers, with their broken pitchers and lamps, put the Midianites to flight, they were in the minority—but they won!

Caleb and Joshua, members of the twelve spies who returned from Canaan, gave their report and found that they were in the minority—but in years to come, they won. Caleb's slogan was, "Give me this mountain." Mount Hebron was his minority inheritance. Although climbing mountains has never been easy, there have always been those few outstanding men, women, and young people who have had the courage and the faith to cast their lot with the minority—and they have won!

I once knew a man who was elected to office. He was very popular in his community but because he would not go along with the county political boss and his underlings, he was not reelected. He was in the minority—but he won. He won because he had a peace of mind that would not have been his had he gone along with the boss who ran the county.

The Bible tells us of many who were of the minority and yet won because, like Moses of old, they "... refused to be called the son of Pharaoh's daughter; Choosing rather to suffer affliction with the people of God, than to enjoy the pleasure of sin for a season ..." (Hebrews 11:24-25).

What better example could we give than the death of Jesus on the cross by Roman soldiers and an evil mob? He seemed very much in the minority on that day, but He won because He was on the side of His Heavenly Father. The minority, in the end, is the majority when it is on God's side.

MASTERS OR SLAVES?

Whatever you love, you are its master. Whatever you hate, you are its slave. Are we masters or slaves?

There are two powers at war in human personalities: the bad and the good, the unwise and the wise, hatred and love.

All evil is built upon hatred. Hatred can always find a mark at which to shoot and a pretense to justify firing. Dictatorships are built upon hatred and fear—democracies upon love and understanding.

Ever since Satan and his angels were cast out of Heaven (Revelation 12:7-9), hatred for God and for those who would serve Him has been the way of evil. Satan is a hater, God is a lover. Arguments won by hatred are only temporary, but crusades won by love are deep and lasting.

A wise man of long ago wrote, "... there is a time to hate... (Ecclesiastes 3:8). There is a time to hate evil, a time to hate sin but to love the sinner. God so loved the world not for what He might gain, but for what He could give.

The Love Chapter (I Corinthians 13) tells us that "love never fails." Hatred always fails though, because it lives only to get and to destroy. But love ever gives; love thinks not of itself.

Mary was six years old. She was in critical condition with a rare disease from which her bright eight-year-old brother John had made a remarkable recovery two years earlier. Mary's only chance for survival lay in receiving a blood transfusion from someone who had previously conquered the disease. Johnny would be the ideal donor.

The family doctor, whom the children knew and trusted, put his hand on Johnny's shoulder and asked, "Johnny, would you like to give your blood for Mary?"

Johnny's lower lip trembled for a moment. Then he looked up at the doctor and replied, "Sure, Doc, I'll give my blood for Mary."

After the transfusion was completed, Johnny, very sober, looked at the doctor and asked, "Dr. Morris, how soon am I gonna die?" Only then did the doctor realize that Johnny had not understood that he was not giving *all* of his blood. The child had believed that giving his blood for his sister had meant that he was giving his life—and he had not hesitated! This is a true story. And it is a true example of what love will do.

At this season of the year out minds turn to the trial of an innocent man. We recall the hatred and violence of the mob, and we mourn the death of Jesus on the cross. We seem to hear anew His words of forgiveness as we reexamine His life of love and sacrifice. We hear again the mob's roar of hatred over against the kind and compassionate avowals of love. Our conclusion is this: If we are to survive as a human race, we must reject any and all conspiracies of hatred and fully commit ourselves to faith, hope, and love.

A NATION'S MEMORY

"We are not here today to glorify war but to honor the dead." Thus I spoke on that Memorial Day many years ago. I have written of the day in my book, *A Time to Remember*.

I had been invited to return to the community where I grew up, and I had accepted. As we gathered around the memorial monument in the cemetery, I looked to the east, far out across the farm where I had been raised. I saw the familiar and peaceful hills, the waving grain, and the contented cattle grazing on the hillsides.

I continued, "Each of these, in whose honor we have gathered, had a right to live out his life. It is with humility that we bow our heads to thank God for them. I pray God that the time will soon come when we shall, as people and races of the world, be able to sit down together around the peace table instead of facing one another across the battlefield." Little did I know that within a few years from that day my own son would be flying away to Korea to engage in another war.

Whenever there are evil minds—minds filled with greed, hatred and jealousy, and lusting for power—wars will continue. We long ago learned that there are no victors in war. We may win the battles, but we do not seem to be able to win the peace.

A line from a poem written following World War I reads, "Take up the battle with the foe." That foe is war itself. The lack of wisdom, the want of real love and understanding, the greed that causes man to lust after too many possessions—these have been and are today the human weaknesses that foster wars.

Judias Iscariot was the disciple who betrayed Jesus, his Master, into the hands of His enemies. The Roman soliders, led by Judas, had entered Gethsemane, where Jesus had been praying, to capture their prize. During this action, Peter drew his sword and cut off the ear of one of the soldiers.

Jesus turned to Peter and said, "Put up again thy sword into his place: for all they that take the sword shall perish with the sword" (Matthew 26:52). No, there can never be lasting peace through war. Yet as long as Satan is loose in the world, there will be wars. The way our Master taught, lived, died, and lived again is the only way of peace.

We come to that day again when we honor those who did what they were called to do. For their sakes, let us pray for the time when we will see the world turn to the great Prince of Peace, Who was willing to give His life that we might have lasting peace.

Jesus gave us the formula: "Blessed are the peacemakers: for they shall be called the children of God" (Matthew 5:9).

THE EXTENDED HAND

As I mention in my book *A Time to Remember*, there were two large apple orchards on the farm where I grew up. When this story begins, it was apple-picking time, and we were busy picking, packing, and loading a railroad car sitting on the siding.

I was about nine years old at the time and was roaming around the freight cars while the apples were being loaded. Then I heard a train whistle. I started to run down the track, looking for an opening between the railroad cars. As I heard the train coming closer, I became frightened. All at once I saw a hand extended from one of the cars on the siding. I reached up and was pulled into the car just as the train went by. I shall never forget the hand that rescued me that day; it belonged to one of my father's crew.

As I was thinking of that incident a few days ago, it occurred to me that many times the extended hand comes just at the right time, when it is most needed.

Matthew tells us of a time when the disciples were in their boat on a storm-tossed sea. Jesus was walking toward them on the water. At His invitation, Peter stepped out of the boat and started to walk toward Him. When Peter saw the waves, he panicked and began to sink. At the plea of Peter, "... Jesus stretched forth his hand, and caught him ..." (Matthew 14:31).

Most of us have experienced periods in our lives when our fears and doubts have almost caused us to give up in despair—and it was then that an outstretched hand of mercy gave us new hope. It may have been at a time when an accident or an illness made us wonder how we were going to get through alive. How comforting it was to have good neighbors come to us with outstretched hands! Or how peaceful we felt when the church came to give us new hope in humanity and a renewed faith in God.

The words of the Psalm-writer are as true today as they were when he wrote, "God is our refuge and strength, a very present help in trouble" (Psalm 46:1). We need not fear. We need only to trust and reach for the hand that is stretched forth to rescue us.

Most of us may have an opportunity—perhaps this very day—to stretch forth our hand in the Master's name to encourage someone who has lost all hope.

I have often wondered where I would be today had not someone stretched forth his hand and let me know that God loves me. It is an act of mercy that makes all the difference between hope and despair, life and death, to those in need of aid and comfort.

TRUE VALUES

"Value of dollar continues to decline ... Inflation plaques our nation's economy ... Decrease in value of social-security benefits troubles senior citizens on fixed incomes ... The cost of living and the fear of dying uppermost in minds of many people." Lately such have been the headlines in our newspapers and the lead stories in the television news reports.

They are serious and sobering statements, and to a great extent they are true. Conditions like these will not go away unless we do something about them.

Will Rogers, self-styled humorist and philosopher, gave us many down-to-earth words of wisdom concerning our country's condition and needs. In 1936, just before he took off by plane on a fatal journey to Alaska, he said, "No bird ever flies so high but what it has to come down to drink." We may chuckle, but we know the words are true.

What is the real value of the *things* we possess? Jesus never condemned riches as such, only as they got in the way of the true values of life.

"Dad," questioned a young man, "how much are you worth?" The father, without hesitation, answered, "Son, my greatest possessions are may family, who trust me, and my faith in God, Who has promised never to leave us nor forsake us." He went on to say, "Sure we own our home, but we shall always be in debt to one another and, above all, to God."

Here was a man who recognized the true values of life. Not that he did not enjoy the material things of life and find satisfaction in seeing them increase for the present and future security of his family. But he had discovered that these possessions by themselves could not bring peace of mind.

This father reminds me of the Psalm-writer who said, "The statutes of the Lord are right, rejoicing the heart: the commandment of the Lord is pure, enlightening the eyes. The fear of the

Lord is clean, enduring for ever: the judgments of the Lord are true and righteous altogether. More to be desired are they than gold, yea, than much fine gold: sweeter also than honey and the honeycomb" (Psalm 19:8-10).

The Psalm-writer goes on to say that "in keeping of them there is great reward." True values are never inflated. They never decrease in value; rather, they become more valuable with the years.

Those people who make true investments—investments in faith, hope, and love, deposited under the wisdom and power of God—will never experience spiritual bankruptcy.

MARCH

Life's Concerns

KEEPING AHEAD OF OUR WORRIES

In my early ministry I made some mistakes that caused me great concern. In fact, I worried about them. Some of those mistakes I could rectify, others I could do little about. They were like feathers scattered to the wind, never to be retrieved again.

One day Uncle Orlo, my good neighbor at a crucial time in my life, said to me as we sat together, "Don, there are two days that we should not worry about. Those days are yesterday and tomorrow."

My trusted friend—who had weathered many of the storms of life and also experienced the sunshine both without and within—counseled me into believing that yesterday is like a canceled check. It has been spent or invested and is gone forever. We have only its memories and its lessons.

Certainly what we did with yesterday has affected today and will influence tomorrow. But we can never reclaim yesterday or turn back time and live it over. We can only try to profit by our mistakes and be thankful for our experiences.

Tomorrow is like a bridge or a mountain that lies ahead of us. We do not cross that bridge or climb that mountain until we reach it. Why spoil today's opportunities with tomorrow's fears?

The counsel of Jesus on this subject concluded with, "Take therefore no thought for the morrow: for the morrow shall take thought for the things of itself. Sufficient unto the day is the evil thereof" (Matthew 6:34). His admonition was that we not be overly anxious about tomorrow, for tomorrow's concerns will take care of themselves if we pray for the wisdom to guide us today.

Life's aging process is like this. Recently I was visiting with a woman who is about to celebrate her ninetieth birthday. Contemplating the event, she said, "One consolation I've had as I've grown older is the realization that one doesn't do it all at once, but only a day at a time."

Only a day at a time! So, if we find ourselves being overly concerned about yesterday and tomorrow, there is only one day left wherein we may find peace—today. If we live with faith, we will have hope for tomorrow, and our disappointments of yesterday will be eased.

The Psalm-writer gives us wisdom for today when he writes, "This is the day which the Lord hath made; we will rejoice and be glad in it" (Psalm 118:24).

I know not what tomorrow will bring, and I cannot turn back the clock of time, but God has given me today. I will rejoice in it and be glad for it. If I can view this day as the day the Lord hath made for me, then when tomorrow comes, I can look back on today and be thankful.

THE AGELESS DISCOVERY

Down on the farm where I grew up, there was a spring. If I were to invite you to go with me to that old spring, you might say, "You have been there so many times. Why not find a new spring?"

My answer would be, "But I not only want to drink again from that old spring, I want to taste the memories of the past. I want to hear the sound of the water as it trickles over the stones worn smooth by the ages. This is the kind of music that thrills and fulfills the spirit."

Come with me, then, to an ageless discovery. It starts with "The Lord is my shepherd." This is a spring that never runs dry. It is not new, but neither is it ever old. It is like the singing of familiar and beloved hymn.

David, and Psalm-writer, reflects upon his early days. His king's sceptre has once again, in memory, become the shepherd's staff. Once more he is the shepherd boy. Although he has reached life's December, June is still in his heart.

The Lord *is*. This is an ageless but ever-fresh discovery. God has always been. Just as the spring was there long before it was discovered, so God was here long before we discovered or recognized Him. The Psalm-writer says, "Before the mountains were brought forth, or ever thou hadst formed the earth and the world, even from everlasting to everlasting, thou art God" (Psalm 90:2).

Long ago on the mountain of Horeb, God spoke to Moses from the burning bush. In calling upon Moses to go back to Egypt and lead the Israelites to freedom, God said that he was to tell them, "I AM hath sent me unto you" (Exodus 3:14).

Since childhood we have quoted from memory the prayer, "The Lord is my shepherd . . ." (Psalm 23:1). This is a *personal* discovery. If God is really to mean anything to us, He must be personal. He is "our Father" in prayer, but He is also "my God."

The Psalmist once again affirms his faith in his God. In the face of enemies, slander, and physical defeat, David says, "But I trusted in thee, O Lord, I said, Thou art my God" (Psalm 31:14).

In the beginning of my ministry, I knew a pastor who was very small in stature but great in inspiration. When he would go to a new church, he could barely be seen over the pulpit lectern.

He would stand as tall as possible and say, "I am a small man, but I have a great God."

We may be small in stature or in talents, but we have a great God. Yes, the Lord is my Shepherd.

PURSUING PATIENCE

On a wall in a good friend's office there hangs a plaque that reads, "Lord, grant me patience, but hurry." As I read those words, I thought: Do we too often pursue patience with such vigor of impatience that we fail to experience it?

When I think of patience, I am reminded of "longsuffering," "waiting," and "calmness." Patience does not mean indifference. We may wait and trust, but we should not be idle or careless while we do so.

John Ruskin, a famous English author, once observed, "There is no music in the rests, but there is the making of music." Those of us who play an instrument or sing know that the "rests" are there for a purpose. So it is in the making of a life. Wait, with patience.

Patience is something one pursues. My father had a bit of wisdom that had to do with our orchards at home on the farm. It also had something to do with life. He advised, "We are not to eat the fruit while it is in the blossom or while it is green."

When Colean, our first granddaughter, was a small child, she used to want to help Grandpa in the flower garden. One day she cried out, "Look, Grandpa, I make the rose bloom!" In trying to make the flower blossom before its time, she spoiled the rose and disappointed herself. "... the trying of your faith worketh patience," James advises us (James 1:3). But he goes on to say that we should not hurry it: "But let patience have her perfect work ..." (James 1:4). This lesson little Colean learned long ago.

A person without patience is like a lamp without a light or a tree without fruit. John Burroughs, an American naturalist, once said that he could grow beautiful tomatoes in sixty days, yet God takes a hundred years to grow a mighty oak.

Patience is prayer, for patience is the gift of the Spirit. "But they that wait upon the Lord shall renew their strength; they shall mount up with wings as eagles; they shall run, and not be weary; and they shall walk, and not faint," so said Isaiah of long ago (Isaiah 40:31).

Walking without fainting tests our patience. Yes, there is a lot of truth in the words on the plaque that reads, "Lord, grant me patience, but hurry."

LIVING EXPECTANTLY

Recently when I was in the post office waiting for the mail to be distributed to the boxes, I found myself in conversation with an elderly friend who said, "I always come each morning to my post-office box expecting."

I have thought of this statement many times since. I too go to the post office or wait for the mail-carrier with expectancy. We may be disappointed at times, but one way of keeping hope alive is to live each day with anticipation.

The expectation of an occasion or a gift is often as exciting as the experience or the present itself. We usually get just about what we expect. If we go to church expecting a blessing, we will more than likely receive it. If we go expecting the service to be dull, we will probably find it dull.

Paul, in writing to the Philippian Christians, used the phrase, "According to my earnest expectation. . ." (Philippians 1:20). He knew that whatever was accomplished through him and through his hopes, expectation would have much to do with it.

First of all, we should begin our day with expectancy. I always pray on awakening, as I lie for a moment in bed, "Thank You, Lord, for letting me see the light of a new day. This is another day that You have made. I know not what is out there, but You know...." A prayer of grateful expectancy at each new dawn will help to make any day a better one.

Again, I find that the spirit of expectancy must be an everyday determination. The farmer's harvest fails. With the spirit of expectancy, he sows once more. The inventor does not give up but faces the problem again. It is reported that Thomas Edison once said, "Every experiment proves to me that it can be done, and I expect to complete it even if it takes a hundred attempts."

Someone asked Babe Ruth, home-run king of baseball, what he thought of when he went to bat. "I expect to hit the ball," was the reply.

"Cast thy bread upon the waters: for thou shalt find it after many days," the wise man wrote many years ago (Ecclesiastes 11:1). If you follow this practical rule, you can expect a happy return from your investment.

Let us determine to live each day with the expectant faith that our lives will be filled with the blessings of our God, from Whom we receive our hopes for tomorrow.

LIFE'S POTENTIALS

"This farm has a far greater potential than meets the eye," the real-estate agent observed. He was showing some friends of mine a property that was up for sale. Looking around, I listened carefully to this enthusiastic salesman who saw possibilities in the land. Having been reared on a farm, I too could see the potential in this farm that to the eye had taken on a depressing mien under the present owner.

A wise schoolteacher of mine, years ago, had a bit of philosophy that she used over and over. It said, "Most of us are capable of more than we produce." She would go on to say that it was her business to help us recognize our potential and to live up to our capabilities.

The disciples of Jesus were not chosen because they were men of great accomplishment but because they were men of great potential. And "Jesus said unto them, Come ye after me, and I will make you to become fishers of men" (Mark 1:17).

Even though I have not lived up to all of my potential, I have often wondered what might have happened to me had not a kindly music teacher encouraged me in my early teens.

I can recall many people, both young and adult, whom I have seen turn their lives over to Christ. We can only guess what they might have become without Him. But I saw the splendid people they became after their lives were channeled in the right direction.

Fred Brock was a young father with a friendly personality, a responsible position, and a promising future. His weakness was drink. He was fast becoming an alcoholic. Fred had a Christian wife and an eight-year-old son who was the pride of his life. I saw in Fred great possibilities, but he was fast dissipating them. Through the influence of that young son and the patience and prayers of his faithful wife, we saw him turn his life over to Christ. Before I left that community, I encouraged Fred to become the Sunday School teacher of a boys' class.

There are those all around us who have great potential for good. They may be just waiting for us to encourage them to channel their lives into the hands of the Great Master, Who knows what we have been and what we can, by His grace, become.

SINGING AT MIDNIGHT

Some of the sweetest songs of all are those that have been written during the midnights of despair. What one of us has not had his midnights of despair? We experience them in times of material distress such as the loss of a job or our savings, or a destructive fire; in times of physical suffering, or when a loved one is taken from us. Some people's lives seem to have been broken by bad breaks. Others have found that often when the doors ahead have been closed, God has opened windows of hope.

We have read that ". . . at midnight Paul and Silas prayed, and sang praises unto God: and the prisoners heard them" (Acts 16:25). These men had been thrown into prison, not for doing evil but for doing good. Although they could have given up in despair, they did not: "They sang praises unto God at midnight."

At midnight we too can sing a song. Long ago someone said, "It is better to light a candle than to curse the darkness."

What might become of our song at midnight? It was said of Paul and Silas, "The prisoners heard them." It has often been true that when we sing, when our night is at its darkest, the prisoners of sorrow and despair hear us and are encouraged.

As World War II was ending, a group of American soldiers, led by their captain, stopped at a little German church whose doors had been barred. They removed the bars and entered. The captain, who had been the church organist back home in Texas, went to the organ. The hymnbook was open to " A Mighty Fortress is Our God."

He sat down and began playing that great hymn so loved by both Germans and Americans. As the strains filled the air, men and women of the little village came in, sat down reverently, and listened. In addition to the American soldiers, there were about twenty German men and women present.

As the captain finished playing, an elderly German came forward with outstretched hands, took the captain by the hands, and said with tears in his eyes, "Mein Bruder! Mein Bruder!" The prisoners had heard the hymn they loved. Their midnight had been brightened. Their church doors were open again.

There are prisoners all about us, waiting for us to sing of our faith at midnight. In so doing, we will find that our own spirits are lifted.

TEMPORARY TOTAL ECLIPSE

It was Monday night, July 5, 1982. The sky was clear. The moon was at its brightest. At 1:00 A.M., July 6, a shadow began to appear on the left-hand side of the moon. It moved slowly across the face of the moon. By 1:30 A.M., the shadow had completely covered the moon.

We watched that phenomenon of God's plan. We knew what it was. We had read that at that very hour the earth would pass between the sun and the moon, causing a total eclipse. Following the event, the moon shone again in all of its brightness. Of course this was not the first time the earth had seemed to put out the moon's light. The eclipse is always only temporary.

The Psalm-writer affirmed his faith when he wrote, "... from everlasting to everlasting, thou art God" (Psalm 90:2). We live in a dependable universe. Things do not just happen by chance. They come to pass as though they were planned—and they were!

Our foreparents knew little, scientifically speaking, about the universe. They used to sing to their children about the cow that jumped over the moon, but they never thought that someday man would travel to that moon. They tilled the soil, planted, cultivated, and harvested with confidence in God, Who had made the heavens and the earth. This was the same moon in whose light Abraham of old went out, strong in his faith in God but not knowing whither he went.

We may disrupt God's plan temporarily, but in the end, God has His way, and we always find that it is for our good. How well we cooperate with Him determines our present and future welfare, and our peace of mind.

A letter I recently received said, "I just lost my grandson to leukemia. His father had it before him. It is difficult for me, at times, to understand. But I still cling to my faith. My comfort comes from the Lord, Who made the heavens and the earth. His plan is not only for a day, but for eternity. Who am I to judge His wisdom? The light of hope seemed to be blotted out at times, but I discovered that it was only temporary. He had not left me. . . ."

Moses, in his final days, encouraged the Israelites with such words as ". . . [the Lord] will not fail thee. . ." (Deuteronomy 31:8). So we can take heart, remembering that His mercy is from everlasting to everlasting unto those who trust Him.

NEVER GIVE UP

Most men and women strive for success in life. Many of them are remembered for their victories in spite of severe handicaps. Few of us reach our goals without courage, faith, hope, and continued determination. A quitter never wins; a winner never quits.

Fanny Jane Crosby was blind from infancy due to a mistake a doctor made in placing hot poultices on her inflamed eyes. In spite of her handicap, she became a prolific hymnwriter. She wrote her first poem at the age of eight, and for eighty years she continued to write. During those years she wrote over eight thousand song poems, and she is especially remembered for about a dozen of them. One of the most familiar is "Blessed Assurance."

The guiding principle of her life became the theme of her songs. That principle was a determined faith in God, Who would not fail her if she did not give up. This theme she expressed in the following words:

Never give up
Trust in the Lord
Sing when your trials are greatest
Trust in the Lord and take heart.

Whether man or woman, those who prevail are those whose

theme in life is, "Never give up; trust in the Lord and take heart."

Hannah of Old Testament days was that kind of faithful and courageous person. Amos R. Wells, author and minister, described her as a "prayer-intoxicated" woman. She had not been blessed with children. She prayed night and day and promised God that if He would give her a son, she would give him to the Lord. Hannah did not give up in despair but gave over to God in trust. Her hopes and prayers were realized, for she became the mother of Samuel, the prophet. As Jane Crosby's hymn goes on to say, "Look on the side that is brightest, Pray and thy path may be clear."

Another story of victory over despair is that of Ruth and Naomi. Death had come to the husbands of Naomi, Ruth, and Orpah. Naomi, the mother-in-law, of the two young women decided in her sorrow to return to her native land. She advised her daughters-in-law to remain in their own country and remarry. Orpah agreed to do so, but Ruth clung to Naomi and said, "Intreat me not to leave thee, or to return from following after thee ... thy people shall be my people, and thy God my God ..." (Ruth 1:16). Is it any wonder, then, that with this kind of love and devotion and in the face of an unknown future, Ruth overcame the obstacles of race prejudice and religious animosity? She never gave up, and today we remember her for her love and loyalty.

As I write this, I am thinking of the countless women and men who, when confronted with what seems like certain defeat, do not give up. Their lives are an encouragement to each of us to "trust in the Lord and take heart."

APRIL

The Hope of Things Eternal

SUNSET—SUNRISE

Sunset and evening star
And one clear call for me....

Alfred Tennyson's poem, "Crossing the Bar," speaks of the "sunset" of life. It does not mean the end of life but the transition of life from one phase to another.

When our Saviour was hanging between heaven and earth on the cross, His enemies thought that this was the end. His days were over. His cry, "... It is finished..." (John 19:30), meant to those who scorned Him that they were finished with Him. They saw only a sunset, but God had already planned a victorious sunrise.

Faithful friends came—in that early morning hour of long ago—to the tomb of their Lord. The sun had set upon their hopes for a victorious king. It was a sad hour for them. Little did they know that their sunset was to be turned into a glorious sunrise.

They could not comprehend the empty tomb, or even the

presence and the words of the angels. But the miraculous appearance of their Lord turned to the sunset of their despair into a sunrise of assurance.

The message of Easter is that life really begins with a resurrection. Jesus had to die that He might prove that He could live again. In so doing, He gave new hope to all who believe in Him. Easter reassures us that we shall again meet those whom we have loved and lost but for a while.

How many times I have read at the funeral service of a loved one the words, "For we know that if our earthly house of this tabernacle were dissolved, we have a building of God, an house not made with hands, eternal in the heavens" (II Corinthians 5:1).

A few years ago I read those words at the memorial service of my youngest sister, Ruby. That day it really dawned on me that this is the message of Easter: An eternal, free-from-pain, assured future with Jesus and those who have gone before us, in a "house not made with hands."

A touching melody and words by William C. Poole sing themselves into our hearts as we say,

> *When I shall come to the end of my way,*
> *When I shall rest at the close of life's day,*
> *When "Welcome Home," I shall hear Jesus say,*
> *O that will be sunrise for me.*

So take heart. Even though life will always have its sunsets, we know that with faith in the eternal Christ, the sunrise that will surely follow is the promise of a new, eternal day.

I BELIEVE

For the past twenty years I have been writing Easter columns. Recently I looked back over the material I had written and studied the title of each column. Afterward I asked myself, "What more can be said? Is there anything new?"

Then I recalled one of the first Gospel songs I learned as a child. I am sure that I did not understand the last verse of that song then as I do now. I think that I know what the author, Katherine Hankey, was thinking when she wrote,

I love to tell the story,
For those who know it best
Seem hungering and thirsting
To hear it like the rest

Although we have heard the Easter story many, many times, the mystery of it all still captures us. How the great miracle on that first Easter morning came about, I cannot explain. It took an act of God to send an earthquake and an angel to roll away the stone from the tomb. Only by the Hand of God could a man who had died at the hands of his enemies arise to greet Mary in the garden.

We are not expected to *explain* the miracle. We are called upon to *proclaim* it. Above all, we must believe it to be a great miracle of God's plan of life eternal.

- I believe in the resurrection of the dead. I see it all about me. I see it in the fields, in the forest, and in the flock. I see it in the springtime, in the seeding, and in the harvest. I see it before me in the physical world.
- I believe in the resurrection of the dead. I see it whenever a life is changed by the transforming Presence of Him who said, "... I am come that they might have life, and that they might have it more abundantly (John 10:10).
- I believe in the resurrection of the dead. I experience it once again as I hear the angel say, "He is not here: for he is risen, as he said. Come, see the place where the Lord lay" (Matthew 28:6).

I am comforted as I stand by the side of a dying loved one for I know, because Christ lives, we shall meet again.

Although the author is unknown, the following lines express my feelings and faith at this season of the year.

My risen Lord, I feel Thy strong protection.
I see Thee stand among the graves today.
I am the Way, the Life, the Resurrection, I hear Thee say,
And all the burdens I have carried sadly
Grow light as blossoms on an April day.
My cross becomes a staff, I journey gladly
This Easter Day.

THE LAST WORD

The old tree still stands. Lightning has struck it. Winds have battered it. More than once it has seemed that the end had come, but each spring it sends out new twigs and blossoms. The old tree will not give up. In spite of all, it is having the last word.

More than two thousand years ago a baby was born in Bethlehem. From the time of Christ's birth to His crucifixion, His enemies tried to destroy Him. When they saw Him die on the cross, they seemed to be satisfied. This was it; they were through with Him. Ah, but they did not know that God always has the last word.

Robert Lowrey, in his poem "Christ Arose," says,

Death cannot keep his prey.
He tore the bars away,
Jesus my Lord.

The celebration of Easter is a time of great joy. It should also be a sobering and sacred occasion. Matthew's account of that first Easter morning tells us that the women "departed quickly from the sepulchre with fear and great joy; and did run to bring his disciples word" (Matthew 28:8).

Easter is more than an argument about immortality. It is a symbol of faith. It is a fact. No fact in this history of the world stands on such firm evidence as does the Resurrection of Jesus. No age of the world has ever needed to believe it more than does ours.

The skeptics say that Easter is old-fashioned, that it is just a story. It could not have happened. Science counteracts this claim by saying that nothing in nature disappears without a trace. Nature does not know extinction; all it knows is transformation.

Every act and occasion in the life of Jesus was the fulfillment of a promise. In that early morning hour, the angel spoke to the sorrowing women: "He is not here: for he is risen, as he said" (Matthew 28:6). The last words were His, and His living Presence was the proof.

The greatest proof that Christ and His plans are invincible is the fact that His enemies could not defeat Him. Our world today, with frustration and trouble in every area of life, needs to know that this Master of life and death is present in our midst to solve each problem that faces us—if we will only let Him.

"How do you know Christ is risen?" an old fisherman along the seashore was asked. His reply was, "Sir, do you see those cottages up there on the cliff? When I am out to sea, I know the sun is risen by the light reflected in their windows. I know Christ is risen when I see His light reflected in the lives around me."

So it is. God has the last word as it is reflected in the lives of all those who believe that Christ is risen.

GOD'S TOMORROW BEGINS TODAY

On a well-lit bulletin borad that stood on the lawn of a beautiful country church, I read the following words: "God's tomorrow begins today." It was Easter Sunday. The first flowers of springtime were in blossom. The church was freshly painted. Everything, including the well-kept cemetery adjacent to the church, seemed to speak of hope.

I entered that church on that beautiful morning. The entire service up to the time of my message spoke of faith and hope. As I began my address, the words on the bulletin board were fresh in my mind. "God's tomorrow begins today," I said. Then I continued, "Is not this the message of Easter?"

As I read again the reports of that first Easter, I asked, "What meaning would all the rest of the Gospel story have if it were not for the Resurrection news?" God's tomorrow really does begin today. The Christian religion begins with the birth of the Saviour and continues with His life and teaching. But the Christian's real faith comes to its climax in the resurrection. This is the victory.

It is this realization that helped a dear friend of mine who was suffering with a terminal disease to say, "I just live a day at a time and trust God for tomorrow." God's tomorrow does not end today. Life with God never ends.

The message of Easter is a message of haste: And "go quickly, and tell his disciples that he is risen from the dead. . . (Matthew 28:7). It is also a message of joy: "And they departed quickly from the sepulchre with fear and great joy; and did run to bring his disciples word" (Matthew 28:8).

Too, the Easter message is the unfailing promise of the ever-present Lord. My mother, like many other women, loved to sing at her work. In doing so, she made her own burden lighter and helped to encourage those around her. One of her favorite songs was, "Peace, Peace, Wonderful Peace," written by Will Cornell. I can hear her now as she sang,

> *What a treasure I have in this wonderful peace,*
> *Buried deep in the heart of my soul;*
> *So secure that no power can mine it away;*
> *While the years of eternity roll.*

To my mother, God's tomorrow begins today. This was what Easter meant to her. I believe that he is singing those beloved words today, along with the great hosts who likewise believed that eternity begins today.

Take heart, dear friend, if despair's dark shadows seem to blot out hope's determined light. The victory of Jesus over death and the grave gives new hope to all who believe that God's tomorrow begins today.

LIFE GOES ON

On the eightieth birthday of the beloved poet Robert Frost, someone asked him what he considered the most significant fact of life. Without hesitation Mr. Frost answered, "The most significant thing is that life goes on."

Every symbol of Eastertime points to this truth. Even the season of spring tells us that there is no death, only resurrection. Life goes on.

Poet John L. McCreery certainly believed that life goes on. He expressed this faith in a poem, part of which goes like this:

> *There is no death! the dust we tread*
> *Shall change, beneath the summer showers*
> *To golden grain, or mellow fruit*
> *Or rainbow-tinted flowers*
> *... And ever near us, though unseen*
> *The dear immortal spirits tread*
> *For all the boundless universe*
> *Is life—there are no dead.*

Is not this what the angels tried to tell those who came to the tomb on that first Easter morning? "... Be not affrighted: ye seek Jesus of Nazareth, which was crucified: he is risen; he is not here: behold the place where they laid him. But go your way, tell his disciples and Peter that he goeth before you into Galilee . . ." (Mark 16:6-7).

The most significant proof that life goes on is the fact that Jesus conquered death and was able to say, "... because I live, ye shall live also" (John 14:19).

Many of us have stood by the bedside of one whom we loved deeply. Our hearts were heavy with grief as we saw that dear person slip away from us. Our hopes for the future seemed to come to an end. But life goes on. As someone has observed, the song is ended, but the melody lingers on. The influence of a life goes on. What someone did and was, like the sound of a trumpet in the hills, will continue to echo throughout the days and years ahead.

If we believe the teachings of Jesus and if we have faith that He rose from the dead, we can take heart. Those whom we have loved and lost for a while have likewise gone before us into a land of life eternal. William Faulkner wrote, "I refuse to accept the end of man." These words express the hope of all men everywhere—the hope that life does not end with our departure from this world.

The experience of that first Easter gives proof to Christians the world over that their hope and faith are not in vain. "For we know," said Paul, the apostle, "that if our earthly house of this tabernacle were dissolved, we have a building of God, an house not made with hands, eternal in the heavens" (II Corinthians 5:1).

THE ENDLESS LIFE

"You cannot keep a rose in the ground if the root is healthy. When God kisses the spot with sunshine and rain, it bursts forth." These words were spoken by Billy Sunday, the great evangelist of the first part of our century. For many years he preached the life, death, and Resurrection of Jesus.

Easter may mean many things to many people, but its central meaning is that death could not hold Jesus. His was an endless life. Death on the cross and a sealed tomb were not obstacles to Him. Those who hastened to the tomb early on that first Easter morning found the stone rolled away.

Someone has said that the stone was rolled away not to permit Christ to come out but to enable the disciples to go in. There they discovered the empty tomb.

Easter's message is not that of an empty tomb but of a risen Christ. The angel's message was not simply, "He is not here ..." but also "... he goeth before you ..." (Matthew 28:6-7).

Yes, He has gone before us—in testing, temptations, courage, sorrow, trial, and death. Now the night is over; the dawn awakens; He lives! The victory is won.

Mary Magdalene, whose past had been forgiven and whose future held hope, came to the tomb of her Master. She had come weeping with an inconsolable sense of loss. She had expected to find her Lord in the tomb. Now she could return with courage and faith. He is not dead, but lives. The graves is not the end. As He lives, we shall live also.

Peter Marshall, one of the great ministers of the twentieth century, believed in Easter. To him, it was more than a celebration or a Spring Festival. He believed and preached the Resurrection of Jesus. In one of his final sermons, he said, "Thank God we have the empty tomb. Death is not a wall, but a door."

It is through this door that many of our loved ones have gone. Many others will follow. It is the way each of us shall go when our lives are finished here. But we can take hope because of Him Who said, "... because I live, ye shall live also" (John 14:19). His is the endless life. Faith in Him can make ours, and those whom we love, endless also.

ROLLING THE STONE AWAY

Sorrow mingled with hope, faith in conflict with doubt. These must have been in the minds of both Mary Magdalene and Mary, the mother of James, as they journeyed to the tomb of their Lord early on that morning of long ago.

One of the questions and fears in their hearts was "...who shall roll us away the stone from the door of the sepulchre?" (Mark 16:3). The soldiers stationed at the tomb could not roll the stone away. The tomb had been sealed by order of Pilate; therefore the soldiers on guard had no authorization. Those faithful women could not roll the stone away. It was too heavy for them.

When the women arrived at the tomb, they discovered that the stone had already been rolled aside "... for the angel of the Lord descended from heaven, and came and rolled back the stone from the door, and sat upon it" (Matthew 28:2).

Most of us do not question the events of that first Resurrection morning. We believe that the stone was not rolled away that Jesus might come out but that those early at the tomb might go in and see that He was not there and hear the words of the angel: "He is not here, for he is risen, as he said. Come, see the place where the Lord lay" (Matthew 28:6).

There are stones in our lives that soldiers of military power cannot remove. There are also stones of fear and doubt that our human strength cannot remove. However, when we continue on our way with the duties of life ever in step with faith, we discover that those stones are rolled away as we come to them.

Most of us have lost loved ones. We have become separated from them by the stone of death. All earthly power cannot roll the stone away. Our own hands are too weak. Then, through faith in the great power of Christ, the risen Saviour, we have peace and consolation in knowing that the stone has been rolled away for us. Instead of death, there is life eternal for that one whom we have loved and lost for a while.

That is the victory of Easter. This is the victorious message of our Lord: "... because I live, ye shall live also" (John 14:19).

THE GOSPEL OF EASTER

Grandma had come to the farm to spend the Easter holidays with her son and his family. She loved the farm, especially in the spring. Early on Eastern morning she was awakened by her eight-year-old grandson. As he pulled at the bed covers, he called out enthusiastically, "Wake up, Grandma, wake up! The world is beginning!"

There was more truth than fiction in the excited words of that little boy. The world really does begin with Easter as far as the Christian faith is concerned.

The Gospel of Easter begins with the dawn. In the yellow light of the oncoming day there walks a lonely, solitary woman. She is on her way to keep an early morning vigil at the tomb. Jesus had done much for this woman whom they called Mary Magdalene. He had lifted her up to a life worth living and had given her a new spirit.

This sad, yet hopeful follower of the Master came to the sepulchre at the rising of the sun. He who sleeps in on Easter morning misses the greatest of all miracles.

The Gospel of Easter also reveals the urgency of *haste*. "And go quickly and tell his disciples that he is risen from the dead; and, behold, he goeth befor you into Galilee; there shall ye see him: lo, I have told you" (Matthew 28:7).

There is no better time to do a good deed than when you have the opportunity. "Go quickly" urged the angel, and the women departed "quickly" and with fear and joy did "run" with the message to the disciples. The good news they could not keep to themselves.

The Gospel of Easter also carries the word *certainty*. Easter is not the story of the end but the revelation of the beginning. On that eventful day Christ transformed death from a sunset to a sunrise. He turned the darkest night into the dawning of a new hope.

Poet Robert Lowrey once wrote a song that says in part:

Up from the grave He arose
With a mighty triumph o'er His foes.
He arose a Victor from the dark domain
And He lives forever with His saints to reign

Because He lives, the crosses we bear are not borne in vain. Because He lives, there is light in the dark valley of death. Because of this, we have the promise that we will be reunited with those whom we love and have lost for a while.

MAY

The Home and Family

BLESS THIS HOUSE

I never sing "Bless This House," written many years ago by Helen Taylor, but that I find the following words have a special meaning to me:

> Bless this door that it may prove
> Ever open to joy and love.

An abode without joy and love may be a house, but it could hardly be called a home. Joy and love are inseparable. They are found in the ingredients that make a house a home.

Edgar Guest, an American poet, speaks our sentiments in his famous poem, "Home." A part of the poems says:

> It don't make any difference how rich ye get to be,
> How much yer chairs an' tables cost, How great yer luxury;
> It ain't home t' ye, though it be the palace of a King,

> *Until somehow yer soul is sort o' wrapped round everything.*

To me, the poet is saying that even though material benefits are necessary, they are not the most important things in a home. The spirit of joy and the warmth of love can make the most humble home a mansion.

The saying, although worn, is still true: "The family that plays and prays together will stay together"

It is good that we have set aside special times such as National Family Week, Mother's Day and Father's Day. They call our attention to the importance and sacredness of the home and family in the life of a nation and its future.

It was at the marriage feast in Cane of Galilee that Jesus performed His first miracle. Here in the warmth of the joy and love that abounded as a new home was established, Jesus turned the water into wine. His very Presence made it a joyful occasion.

These days we hear much about equal rights. What one of us does not believe in equal rights for all? With equal rights, however, comes equal responsibility. No family can be at its best, or enjoy peace and harmony, unless each member accepts his or her responsibilities.

Paul, the apostle, writing to his good friend Timothy and commending him for his dedication, says, ". . . When I call to remembrance the unfeigned faith that is in thee, which dwelt first in thy grandmother Lois, and thy mother Eunice; and I am persuaded that in thee also" (II Timothy 1:5). The faith that Timothy possessed did not come to him by bequest, but by conquest. However, the examples that his mother and grandmother set before him had much to do with the life that was his.

So we pause at this season of the year to pay honor to those parents who set lights in the windows of faith and courage—and then kept them burning. We thank God for our forefathers and their examples of love and perseverance. By His grace, may we set equal examples for those who come after us.

FOOTPRINTS

"Fingerprints are the means by which we track our criminals; footprints are the marks by which we follow our heroes," Henry Wadsworth Longfellow advised. We may each choose by what manner we care to be remembered.

The interesting fact about footprints is that they remain long after we are gone. Some people leave footprints in the sands of time; others leave a heelmark.

In what we call the Faith Chapter of the Book of Hebrews, we read of the faith of Abel, one of the first sons of Adam and Eve. He met a tragic death at the hands of his brother, Cain. But even though Abel met his death early in life, he had lived long enough that it was said of him: "By faith Abel . . . being dead yet speaketh" (Hebrews 11:4). This kind of remembrance might be called the immortality of influence.

Influence, good or bad, is something we leave behind us. It is the continuing effect of a person's existence even though he or she has passed from the scene of physical presence.

As we walk among the burial spots at this season of the year, we realize that they are sacred places to us. They are sacred not because those whom we have loved are there but because of our memories of those dear people—memories that will ever be in our hearts.

Many of our beloved had the opportunity to live out their time. There are others, however, above whom the stars and stripes wave, who did not have that opportunity. Many of these brave ones are buried in unmarked graves, some even on foreign soil. Wherever they are, we know that to many of us like Abel, they, continue to speak after their death. These memories are part of the foundation upon which America stands.

Carl Sandburg, an American poet and biographer, once said, "If America forgets from whence she has come; if her people lose sight of what brought them along; if we listen to the mockers and the deniers, then we will begin to decay into desolation."

Our determination for this season of the year should be that, by God's help, we hold sacred the deeds of those who gave their lives in service and love. Let us here resolve that we too will be faithful so that those who come after us may walk in our footprints as we follow the One, Jesus Christ, Who lives forever in our hearts.

THE ART OF TOUCHING

There are many childhood memories that are still vivid to me today. Among them are those nights when I would awaken with a headache and be unable to go back to sleep. One of my most treasured memories is that of a concerned mother coming to my bedside and laying her hand softly upon my forehead. There was healing in the touch, mainly because it was the gentle touch of a mother who loved and cared.

There are so many people around us who need the touch of love, or who need to practice that touch. One of the most significant marks of the ministry of Jesus was His compassionate love. The Gospel according to Mark tells us that "... they bring a blind man unto him, and besought him to touch him" (Mark 8:22). Jesus possessed the art of touching. It was a Divine power. Think of the many times it is reported that Jesus touched someone—and a healing occurred.

There are those who use their fists in attempting to solve the problems of the world. Under this plan, the problems always get worse instead of better. It is only when we learn the touch of love, compassion, and understanding that we see our problems begin to be solved.

One of the finest hospital nurses I know has dedicated her life's work to the healing touch—relying not only on medicine but also on the power of love. Her patients know that she is concerned about them, and they respond to her capable, compassionate touch.

The ministry of healing often uses many hands. Like the surgeon who said to me, "I operate, God heals." When they brought the man sick with palsy and let him down through the roof that Jesus might heal him, Mark said that they brought him on his bed "borne by four." And "When Jesus saw their faith. . ." (Mark 2:5), He healed the man. But each of the four men shared with Jesus in the healing touch of this unfortunate victim.

A dear, retired pastor once said to me in the beginning of my ministry, "Don, don't ever forget that if you want to help people, you must let them know that you really care for them." He was right. This caring is so important to the art of truly touching the lives of others.

Reach out. Place your hand and concern on somebody else's life today. That person will not only be helped, but in the end you will receive more than he.

A HOUSE, OR A HOME?

The first house I remember is the place in which I spent my early childhood. I loved that house not because it was a palatial residence, which it was not, but because my parents made it a home. Many ingredients are necessary to the formula for a happy home.

One of those ingredients is *patience*. I look back now and realize that parents do not bring nine children into the world, as mine did, and rear eight of them without acquiring patience. My parents not only practiced patience, they taught the value of "waiting" to their children.

Another element that goes into the making of a house a home is *encouragement*. Encouragement tells us to hold one another's hands through difficult times and to applaud one another's sincere efforts. What one of us has not felt the warmth of an encouraging hand? Sometimes correction is necessary, and it does much good—but encouragement does more.

Many tears go into the making of a house a home. Tears of pain, tears of disappointment, and, of course, tears of joy. Paul tells us to "Rejoice with them that do rejoice, and weep with them that weep" (Romans 12:15). Sharing our tears helps to bring the family closer together.

"How is everyone at your house?" I asked five-year-old Billy as he sat on the front doorstep.

Billy looked up and lamented, "We all have a pain in Jackie's stomach."

A sincere and sympathetic tear is good, but we must do even more than weep with them that weep, for of all the ingredients that combine to make a house a home, there is one that leads the rest. Without it, the others would not function. That powerful element is Love. Love keeps hope alive.

In the great Love Chapter we read that love "Beareth all things, believeth all things, hopeth all things, endureth all things" (I Corinthians 13:7).

Henry Van Dyke, author and pastor, observed that "Every house where love abides is surely home, for there the heart can rest."

So as we pause to observe National Family Week and Mother's Day, it is good to remember Henry Van Dyke's poem:

Blessed is the house that's home,
Where God Himself is known,
Where families that have learned to share
Will find a Home awaiting there.

THE PERFECT MAN

Many years ago as a young pastor, I was called to conduct the funeral service of an aged Civil War veteran. Cap Franklin was his name. He had been through many battles, and in his declining years he loved to tell of his experiences. He had been a faithful soldier. He had also been a faithful husband.

At his death, his companion of many years asked that I use the words, "Mark the perfect man," as the theme at his funeral. I am sure that any husband would be happy to know that his wife would make such a thoughtful request.

A perfect man. What makes a perfect man or woman? One hopeful woman once said that her idea of a perfect husband was one who remembers your birthday but forgets your age. Saint Augustine said, "This is the very perfection of a man, to find out his own imperfection."

The farmer's goal may be a perfect furrow; the housewife's goal a perfect house. The athlete may strive for a perfect game. All of these and many more may strive for perfection, and well they should. No man reaches higher than his goal.

No, I did not point to Cap Franklin when I said, "Mark the perfect man." As good a man as he was, he was not perfect. I did, however, point to the One Whose life Cap Franklin exemplified.

The writer of the Psalms said, "Mark the perfect man, and behold the upright: for the end of that man is peace" (Psalm 37:37). Jesus, in His Sermon on the Mount, said, "Be ye therefore perfect, even as your Father which is in heaven is perfect" (Matthew 5:48). As good and worthy of being called perfect as Jesus was, He pointed not to Himself but to His Father as the true mark of perfection.

The artist had worked at his easel for many hours. Both night and day he toiled away. The picture must be perfect if he would win the coveted prize. Weary but determined to make it complete, he tried once more. His strength of mind and body failed him, and he dropped off to sleep. And as he slept, the master artist came. With a stroke of the brush here and there, the picture was finished.

When the young artist awoke, he gazed at it in amazement and heard the master teacher say, "Take heart, my son. Never give up. Remember, the virtue lies in the struggle, not in the prize."

The best advice I ever received was, "Strive, by God's help, to do your best, and leave the rest to Him Who will make perfect the struggle in His own time."

SING—SMILE—PRAY

Sing and smile, and pray,
That's the only way.
If you sing and smile, and pray,
You'll drive the clouds away.

Those words are a part of a little song composed by my good friends, Virgil and Blanche Brock many years ago. Often I have found in these lines a tried and true formula for the dispelling of the clouds of life or for giving a cloud a silver lining.

Singing is an outlet for our feelings. By it we express our faith. It also helps us to eliminate our fears. If we sing a song as we go along, it will lighten our burdens and right a wrong.

Each of us has found, however, that it takes courage to keep a song on his lips when he has a sob in his heart. The Psalm-writer has said, "And he hath put a new song in my mouth..." (Psalm 40:3). What is the source of this song? It is a gift from God. Its source is like a spring that never runs dry. This song does not change with the seasons.

The song to which I have referred also said, in another verse, "Smile the clouds away, Night will turn to day." A smile that lights the face will also warm the heart, not only our own but that of someone who is hoping for a smile instead of a frown. A smile cannot be bought, begged, or stolen. It is of no earthly account until it has been given away. It is difficult to conceal the thoughts of the heart. A smile is the reflection of a cheerful heart.

Many years ago I had a radio program in which I used the song, "Sing, Smile, and Pray," as my theme song. One day a letter arrived from southern Ohio in which the writer said, "There have been times when I couldn't sing or smile the clouds away, but there has never been a time that I couldn't pray the clouds away."

The disciples of Jesus, noting the effect that praying had on the life of their Master, came to Him saying, "... Lord, teach us to pray, as John also taught his disciples" (Luke 11:1). It was then that Jesus gave to them the pattern for all prayers.

Someone has said that we should pray as though all things depended upon God and work as though all things depended upon us.

Many of the clouds of life have been given a silver lining through dedicated faith in prayer. So, my friends,

*If you sing and smile, and pray,
you'll drive the clouds away.*

HOME

Some time back, I had a part in a family-life conference. At the beginning of the conference, I wrote one word on the blackboard. That one word was "Home." Then I asked the group what the first thing they thought of was when as they saw the word.

The following is a short—but meaningful—list of responses: family, memories, security, love, understanding, influence, guidance, fear, and discipline.

As we discussed the reasons for our different associations, the woman who had mentioned "fear" explained her feeling. "I grew up in a home where I had an alcoholic father," said this mother of three children. She went on to tell of the abuse inflicted upon her mother, her brothers, and her sisters by her father when he was under the influence of alcohol. "After I was grown and left home, my father's life was changed. God touched him through the ministry of a man who won his confidence." She went on to say, "But those formative years were not lost. My mother did all she could to keep the home together, and I do thank God for what He did with and for my father in his later years."

I have often wondered what our children think of when the word *home* is mentioned. While most of us do not remember home as a place where we had everything we wanted, we likely had all that we needed. Some of us may remember experiencing fear in childhood, but most of us can recall love and understanding—along with doses of discipline as needed.

In this day, when the breakdown and decay of the home as we once knew it is evident, we need to reevaluate our priorities and redefine the place of the home in our society. Can our civilization endure under modern trends? Shall our children become pawns of the state?

Like many of you, I am thankful for what the home still means to our world's present and our future hopes. With Paul, we can say, "For this cause I bow my knees unto the Father . . . Of whom the whole family in heaven and earth is named" (Ephesians 3:14-15). The family is God's creation. The Psalmwriter wrote, "God setteth the solitary in families . . ." (Psalm 68:6).

God spoke to Abraham of His hope for His creation when He said, ". . . in thee shall all families of the earth be blessed" (Genesis 12:3).

Once again we pause to show gratitude to God for the homes that have influenced our lives and for the parents who have given us their love and faith. As we do so, let us pray that we may not only memorialize the home of the past but that we may dedicate anew our efforts toward a more meaningful present and helpful future for our young people. "Home" is still one of the best words in the world.

POWER

"Dad, that's power!" This was the enthusaistic voice of our ten-year-old son as we rode along in the family car. We had been waiting for the red light to change to green. As it did so, a motorcycle sped away with a loud burst of noise. Our family Buick went on its silent way. To Martel, the noise of the motorcycle denoted power.

Power and noise seem to be synonymous to many people these days. We have become so accustomed to noise that silence almost seems to indicate weakness.

"I never slept a wink last night." Those are the words of a man born and reared in New York City who had come out to his brother's farm in Ohio to visit for a few days. He was so used to the clamor of the city that the quietness of his brother's farm kept him awake!

"How do you stand in with nothing ever going on here in the country?" the city man asked his farmer brother.

The brother answered, "Come out with me tonight under the stars. Catch the scent of the apple blossoms bursting into bloom. Hear the corn growing and its blades rustling in the breeze. Listen to the singing of the frogs in the pond and the trickling of the water in the brook."

That farmer brother was right: *Listen.* Whenever we *listen* to God at work in His universe we hear sounds of power. The Psalm-writer reflects on this as he writes, "Be still, and know that I am God . . ." (Psalm 46:10).

Many of us have discovered that God works in mysterious ways His wonders to perform. Often He manifests His power as we wait quietly before Him. Elijah of Old Testament days discovered this. Up on the mountain there was a great strong wind and an earthquake, but God was not in these. "And after the earthquake a fire; but the Lord was not in the fire: and after the fire a still small voice" (I Kings 19:12).

How true the words, "But they that wait upon the Lord shall renew their strength. . . " (Isaiah 40:31). Waiting means trusting, praying—and listening.

A church stands on the busy circle of a city that I have visited for many years. Progress seems to have passed it by, and many tall buildings have grown up around it. The little church stands in the shadow of man's advancement. But there is a sign on the lawn that reads, "Come in, rest, and pray." In the stillness of that sacred place, I, like many others in similar quiet places, find the true source of the power that sustains and keeps us.

It has ever been and will ever be so.

BEING UNDERSTANDING

*If we could but draw back the curtains
That surround each other's lives,
. . . Often we would find it better,
Purer than we judge we could,
We would love each other better if we only understood.*

The above lines are from a poem entitled "If We Understood." The author is unknown, but the words are worth pondering. The poem goes on to say:

*Could we judge all deeds by motives,
See the good and bad within,
Often we should love the sinner
All the while we loathe the sin.*

There is an old Indian proverb that, as I recall, says, "I will not judge another until I have walked three days in his moccasins."

Through the years some of my most helpful friends have been those who have been charitably understanding with my misunderstood actions. Many of us have been encouraged by understanding friends who have judged our errors with patient charity.

Solomon of Old Testament days prayed, "Give therefore thy servant an understanding heart to judge thy people, that I may discern between good and bad..." (I Kings 3:9). This prayer still has meaning for our day and for each of us. Praying for an "understanding heart" is seeking not only for wisdom but for compassion.

One of the characteristics of Jesus was His compassion. He had sympathy, or pity, for those who were unfortunate. He did not condone sin, but He had compassion for the sinner.

Our anonymous poet goes on to say:

Could we know the powers working
To o'erthrow integrity,
We should judge each other's errors
With more patient charity.

In the Sermon on the Mount, Jesus counseled His hearers to "Judge not, that ye be not judged. For with what judgment ye judge, ye shall be judged: and with what measure ye mete, it shall be measured to you again" (Matthew 7:1-2). My sainted mother had a saying that she practiced daily: "If you can't say anything good about a person, don't say anything." There were times when her quiet tongue was far more effective than words. Her charitable spirit was experienced by all who knew her.

"Because you prayed for me rather than condemning me, because you went out of your way to show your concern for me and my family and had patience with me, our home is once again as it used to be. God loves us, and you helped us to see this." Those are the words of a man of my experience from out of the past.

The life of one who practices "an understanding heart" is indeed rich in Heavenly dividends, particularly in the joy he experiences when he sees those to whom he has shown compassion grow in renewed hope.

WHAT IS A MASTERPIECE?

I cannot paint a picture
Of the leaves a turning red
Nor can I write a poem or a song
That the world for long would sing.
I may not be an artist
But I can bake a loaf of bread.

This bit of verse was handed to me recently. The author is unknown to me, but the lines express the sentiments of most of us who feel that we have accomplished so little in life.

Captain Bill Knepper used to come often to our farm when I was a youngster. I am not sure what war he was in, but it pleased him when we called him captain. He seemed to have a way of arriving just before mealtime. He was not much of a hand with the ax or the pitchfork, but at the table he could do the work of two men.

"Minnie," he would say to my mother without looking up from his plate, "this dinner is a masterpiece if ever I saw or tasted one. I'll thank you for another of those blue-ribbon biscuits."

My mother, bless her heart, was not carried away by all this. But as I look back, those meals *were* masterpieces.

Naturally we think of a masterpiece as a work of art by an artist who became famous after he was gone or as a great piece of sculpture that has withstood the criticism of time. But are not masterpieces to be found all around us? Might it not be the accomplishment of baking a loaf of bread? Or of developing an outstanding rose? Could it be the growing of blue ribbon corn, or the raising of 4-H outstanding steer?

What is a masterpiece? To me it is doing your best with the talent God has given you. Is not the helping of that child to grow into an honest, upright youth similar to the creation of a masterpiece?

The Gospels do not tell us as much as we would like to know about the childhood and young manhood of Jesus. We are sure, however, that the influence of the mother of Jesus had much to do with the fact that the Gospel-writers are able to say, "And Jesus increased in wisdom and stature, and in favour with God and man" (Luke 2:52).

Many years ago, God took a rough, cursing captain of a slave ship, John Newton, and changed him into a man who could write:

Amazing grace!
How sweet the sound,
That saved a wretch like me

John Newton became one of God's masterpieces.

It is not what we have been but what we can become, by God's grace and power, that counts. God does not change our talents. He redirects them so that whatever we are, with whatever we have, we may become a blessing to others and a glory to His name. This is the making of a masterpiece.

THE AFTERGLOW

It was a cold winter evening. I sat deep in nostalgic musing by the fireside, leafing through a magazine that comes regularly to our home. I came across a scene illustrative of long-ago times, and it brought back many fond memories of my childhood days.

As I sat there lost in recollection, the wood in the fireplace burned low. I watched the glowing embers and realized then that those happy times were now but the afterglow of days gone by.

Why is it that the singing of some old song so often strikes a harmonious chord in our hearts? It is because of the memories it stirs within us. Why is it that those experiences must sometimes age before they come to mean much to us? Is it because the value of certain things becomes more apparent with the passing of the years?

It is frequently true that a man or a woman is not really appreciated until he or she has gone from this world. After they have left us, the wisdom of their words and the example of their lives take on greater meaning. It is the afterglow of their lives that lingers on.

The poet and the composer seldom become famous until after they are gone. They are often misunderstood in life but revered in death. Sometimes our own parents' judgment is not respected in life but is hallowed in death. It is the afterglow of their lives that lingers on to bless their memory.

A dear friend of mine gave twenty-five years to his chosen vocation as a public-school teacher. At the very height of his career as a high-school counselor, his earthly life was terminated in an automobile tragedy. At the time of his funeral, hundreds came to show their love and respect. Many of these were students who had benefited from his wise counsel. Someone was heard to say that the influence of his life would live or forever in the lives of those whom he had taught.

Jesus lived for thirty-three years in this world. He never wrote a book; He never made a trip around the world, nor did He own any property. He was despised by many and rejected by others. He has, however, influenced more people by His life and teaching than any other person who has ever lived.

His life has inspired the writing of many, many books. He has traveled around the world, and his name is known by every race. The afterglow of His life has influenced more people for good than will ever be known. He has given us a light that will brighten our pathway throughout eternity. He has inspired countless men and women to give their lives in service for others—the kind of service that seeks not the applause of man but the approval of God.

Most of us will never become famous for our achievements. We can, however, give of ourselves in such a way that our lives may live on in the afterglow.

Mother often baked homemade bread on churning day. She would open the oven door of the wood-burning kitchen range and say, "Oh, Donald, how good a slice of this warm bread is going to taste with some of that butter you are churning. I'll fix you a slice as soon as you have finished." That promise was enough to keep me persisting to the end of the task.

As I look back now after all these years, I realize how much like life was the experience of churning the butter in those days long ago. Paul, in writing "Therefore let us not sleep..." (I Thessalonians 5-6) to the early Christians of the Galatian Church, is saying to us today that we cannot expect to reap the harvest of a life well invested if we grow weary and faint by the wayside.

Jesus often spoke of the fruits of persistent living. Once this Master of wisdom counseled, "... men ought always to pray, and not to faint..." (Luke 18:1).

God has promised never to leave us nor forsake us. Therefore, don't faint, pray ... don't faint, trust ... don't faint, keep on keeping on.

With Him, all things are possible.

THE LIGHT IN THE WINDOW

One of the memories of my childhood and youth that I have treasured through the years is that of the light in the window at home. The night was never too dark or the evening too late but when it was there, shining through the trees in the orchard. The anticipation I always felt as I neared home, heightened by the warmth of a mother who cared and a family who shared, was never disappointed.

This season of the year our thoughts turn to National Family Week and Mother's Day. As I meditate upon this special time, I think again of the light in the window at home. He or she who does not have a childhood memory of the faithful light of love, understanding, and hope has missed one of life's greatest treasures.

Long after I left the home of my youth, I continued to receive a card in the mail each week. It was another light along the way. The card always ended with the words, "Remember, I'm praying for you." Mother was been gone these twenty-five years, but the light she set in the window long ago still shines.

Thelma and I set a light in the window of our companionship and home in July, 1925. It has been our hope and prayer through the years that that light may bring memories of encouragement, hope, and love not only to our son and his family but to many others who have glimpsed its rays.

The parents, the families, and the homes that leave lasting, positive memories behind them are those who take the words of Jesus seriously. Speaking to the multitude, He said, "Ye are the light of the world. A city that is set on an hill cannot be hid" (Matthew 5:14).

Sir Harry Lauder, a Scottish singer, was thrilled as a child to watch the lamplighter go about his task, and he observed, "I could always tell where the lamplighter was by the stream of light he left behind him." The best proof of the steadying influence of a home may be seen in the stream of light it radiates as a beacon to guide us.

There has never been a time when the world, with all its uncertainty, has needed the prayers, the Godly courage, and the light of hope in the windows of our homes more than it does now. I pray that we may not fail.

THE HEAD OF THE HOUSE

It was a cold February morning. I had spent the night with my aging parents, and now we were sitting at the breakfast table. The coffee pot was emitting its aroma as it simmered on the back of the kitchen stove. The tea kettle was singing a lazy tune of warmth and satisfaction.

As Mother and Dad and I ate and visited, my attention was drawn to the mantel on the wall when the old clock struck six. As I looked, I saw the motto beside the clock that had been there for as long as I could remember.

I knew the words on that motto by memory: "Christ is the Head of this house; The unseen Guest at every meal; The silent Listener to every conversation." My brothers and sisters and I had come under the influence of those words because we had parents who believed in them and practiced them.

Our parents are gone now, but not their influence. I ask myself: Will our son and grandchildren be similarly influenced because Thelma and I look to Christ as the Head of our house?

Joshua, the leader of the Israelites as they entered Canaan, was delivering his final address to his people. He warned them of the hardships ahead but encouraged them with visions of new opportunities. He urged them to decide whom they would serve: ". . . choose you this day whom ye will serve; whether the gods which your fathers served that were on the other side of the flood; or the gods of the Amorites, in whose land ye dwell: but as for me and my house, we will serve the Lord" (Joshua 24:15).

Freedom of choice is still one of our individual freedoms, and it is a solemn one. The success or failure of our future, and the future of those whom we may influence, depend on our making the right decisions now. When our beloved nation was founded, its leaders confessed their dependence upon "Divine wisdom." George Washington affirmed this dependence when he said, "The blessing and protection of Heaven are at all times necessary."

Benjamin Franklin, senior member of the Constitutional Convention of 1787, spoke with wisdom and concern to the wrangling delegates as he observed, "God governs in the affairs of men. And if a sparrow cannot fall to the ground without His notice, is it probable that an empire can rise without His aid?" Dr. Franklin was echoing the wisdom of the Psalm-writer who said, "Except the Lord build the house, they labour in vain that build it . . ." (Psalm 127:1).

Whether it be a nation, a house, or an individual, our welfare is safe and secure only as we make Him, our Lord, the Head of our house.

PERSISTENT PERSUASION

Recently I sat with some friends at a table in a barn that had been converted into a restaurant. While watching for our food to be served, I noticed that many implements in the barn were of the era of my childhood.

Near me there was an old butter churn just like the one I used to operate. It was one of those keg-type churns on a frame with a crank on the side that one turned to revolve the churn. I am sure that many readers will remember what it was like.

As I recall, it took a lot of persistence on my part, as well as determined persuasion by my mother, to keep me turning that churn until the butter was formed. My mother knew her Bible and often used an example to illustrate her point. One of the verses she called upon to persuade us not to give up on any chore was the one that she quoted on churning day.

"How much longer, Mom?" I would plead. "Isn't it time for the butter to come?"

After my pleading and complaining, I would hear my mother say, "And let us not be weary in well doing: for in due season we shall reap, if we faint not" (Galatians 6:9).

JUNE

Youth and the Future

IF I WERE YOUNG AGAIN

"It is better to build youth than to mend men." Such were the words that caught my attention as I was handed the program of a thater-and-son banquet at which I was to speak one evening.

My subject was to be "If I Were Young Again." The words at the top of the program were much in keeping with the occasion and the subject.

My father had a saying that has stayed with me through the years. He reasoned, "It is easier to break a colt than to change the habits of a horse." I do not know that he had ever seen the line quoted above, but he had five sons. He too was young once. He was talking from experience.

I suppose there are times when we all look back and say, "If I had my life to live over, I would do some things differently." On the other hand, if we had our lives to live over and had not the benefit of the experience that has been ours, we no doubt would make other mistakes—just as we make mistakes in our youth. Even though this may be true, if I were young again,

I would endeavor to form good habits. As a tree is trained, so will it grow. The same is true of our lives.

Someone has observed that first we make our habits, then our habits make us. Habit is either the best of servants or the worst of masters.

I wept with a father whose son, not yet eighteen, had taken his life and left a note saying, "It has gotten me, life is finished, there is no future for me." Thousands of young people are to be pitied, not condemned, that drugs and other dangerous habits have confused them into believing that this is all that life is about.

If I were young again, I would plan for the future. Unless a tree has borne blossoms in the spring, one need not look for fruit in the fall. What a wonderful thing it is that in our youth we have the vigor and the enthusiasm to plan for the future. If I were young again, I would place my faith in God, Who is wisdom, power, and love. The wise man of long ago wrote, "Remember now thy Creator in the days of thy youth..." (Ecclesiastes 12:1).

I believe that our Creator has a plan for every life He brings into the world. The earlier in life we give Him an opportunity to help us lay our foundations, the richer will be our future.

"In all thy ways acknowledge him, and he shall direct thy path" (Proverbs 3:6). This is good counseling for any age. It is exceptionally good for our youth.

SATISFACTION GUARANTEED

"Satisfaction Guaranteed—Is Our Aim." Such were the words that I found at the bottom of a letterhead belonging to a long-established and successful business concern.

Most of us have learned, however, that there are certain provisos with every guarantee. This is true in all walks of life— the material, the physical, and the spiritual.

Recently our granddaughter Colean came into possession of the old clock that has stood on the floor in our home for the past fifty-three years. The old clock had been the faithful guardian of time through all the hours of those years.

Before we loaded the clock into Colean's car, she asked, "Grandpa, what directions can you give me so my clock will continue to run and keep time as it has for you and Grandma?"

My answer was, "Colean, there are three things you must not forget. First, be sure that the clock is level. A clock with a pendulum will not continue to run if it is out of balance."

This is truly a parable of life. I was an adult before I heard much about balanced rations. But as I look back now, I thank God for parents who taught us that life's values must be kept in balance if our future was to be secure. "Prove all things; hold fast that which is good" (I Thessalonians 5:21). So wrote Paul long ago. These words are as urgent today as they were when written. Testing before accepting is a good rule for keeping life in balance.

The second thing I said to Colean was "Don't forget to wind the clock." How many times I had risen in the night to wind that faithful clock as it was struggling to strike the hour. A German clock-maker of my acquaintance once said, "A tight spring is power."

Praying is the winding of our spiritual clock. We would do well not to be lax in the winding process. It was Paul who advised his spiritual son Timothy, "Study to shew thyself approved unto God, a workman that needeth not to be ashamed, rightly dividing the word of truth (II Timothy 2:15). My German clock-master friend was right.

Last, but not least, I said, "Enjoy your clock." Joy is the outcome of accepting and applying the provisos of the formula for the good life. In the final evening with His disciples before His trial and death, Jesus said, "These things have I spoken unto you, that my joy might remain in you, and that your joy might be full" (John 15:11).

Joy is not always an audible exuberance but often an inward experience that expresses itself in quiet action. It comes to us when we have kept our lives in balance and our spiritual spring firmed with prayer.

HANDICAPS

It was a chilly, wet morning after a rainy night. As I reached a busy street corner, I came upon a newsboy whose papers were stored behind a post in front of the bank. Just ahead of me was a local businessman. As he stopped to get his regular morning paper, he greeted the boy with, "Well, Jake, how are things this morning?"

"Can't complain, Mr. Jordon, and I wouldn't if I could," replied the boy. Then, his crutch under one arm, he turned to the next customer, who was me. As I greeted him, I did not ask him about his religion. I was convinced that here was a person revealing one of the true marks of faith and courage. He had overcome his handicap.

The attitude with which we face life—its hopes, its disappointments, and its handicaps—determines not only our own future but often that of those around us. Turn in any direction, even to your own mirror, and you are likely to see someone with a handicap, some worse off than others. Handicaps can make us bitter—or better.

"It is not what you have lost but what you have left that counts," a retired public-school teacher said to me one day. She had lost her eyesight but had not given up. She went on to say, "I may be blind, but God has given me a keen sense of touch."

Samson, the Bible's Hercules, had a handicap. It was his strength. It overcame him. The rich young man who came to Jesus inquiring what good thing he might do to inherit eternal life had a handicap. He was one of great possessions, and he turned away from Jesus. He could not bring himself to sell what he had, give to the poor, and follow Jesus.

Zacchaeus, the Big Little man of whom Luke 19 speaks, had a handicap: He was short of stature. He was at a disadvantage in the crowd that flocked to see Jesus. But because he was tall in courage, he overcame his handicap and became the host at dinner for Jesus that day.

It was Helen Keller who, with more than her share of handicaps—being blind, deaf, and mute—overcame her disabilities. She once said, "We do not become strong by what we get, but by what we become."

Through courage and faith we can, like the apostle Paul, hear our Lord say, ". . . My grace is sufficient for thee: for my strength is made perfect in weakness" (II Corinthians 12:9). We too can be overcomers of our handicaps.

KEEPING ALIVE

"Lord, keep me alive as long as I live," prayed a thoughtful Scotchman long ago. As I think of it, that is a good prayer for each of us. Keeping alive for as long as we live is the hope of most of us.

Moses, the leader of Israel out of its days of slavery in Egypt and on its journey through the wilderness, knew that his days were numbered. He was not only his people's leader but the mouthpiece of God, responsible for the future welfare of His people.

". . . I have set before you life and death, blessing and cursing: therefore choose life, that both thou and thy seed may live . . ." (Deuteronomy 30:19). Thus spoke God through Moses to the hopeful, yet fearful, children of Israel. Their choice of life determined not only their future but the welfare of those who followed after them.

It is just as true today that if we would keep alive for as

long as we live, we should make the most of today. I have only one life to live. I shall not pass this way again.

If we would keep alive, we would do well to live our lives in concern for others. The happiest folk I have known have been those who lived with the welfare of others first in mind. One of the finest things they said about Jesus was that He went about doing good.

If we would stay alive, we would also do well to invest our lives in eternal things. It was William James, an American philosopher, who impressed upon his students the need to invest their lives in deeds that would outlast them.

In our plans and hopes for our lives, we must be ever mindfull of Who holds the key to life. William Ernest Henley, an English poet, suffered much but kept up his courage. He wrote, "I am the master of my fate; I am the captain of my soul." This can be true for us too only as we make the right choices in life.

When Jesus announced His purpose in coming to this world, He said, "... I am come that they might have life, and that they might have it more abundantly" (John 10:10). If we would keep alive for as long as we live, we would do well to remember He Who holds the key to all that is worthwhile in our lives.

GIVE ME THIS MOUNTAIN

Two men who had been good friends for years were vacationing together. One was an artist, the other a timber merchant. They had camped for the night in a beautiful valley between two mountains. As the sun sank behind the mountain to the west, it cast a colorful afterglow on the wooded hills to the east.

The men began to evaluate the scene. The artist commented on what a wonderful picture it would make. The timber merchant speculated on how much lumber could be cut from the trees that covered the mountainside. Both of these men viewed the mountain through different eyes, but each saw possibilities in it. Each was saying, "Give me this mountain, and I'll use it."

Whether we are an artist, a timber merchant, a scientist, or a mere traveler, mountains may present problems—or opportunities. It all depends on how we view them. Life's mountains too can be either a challenge or a stumbling block.

There are at least three things we can do with a mountain. We can climb it; we can enjoy it; and we can use it.

There is a story of Old Testament days that has always held my interest. It concerns two faithful Israelites, Joshua and Caleb. The children of Israel, in God's good time and by His grace, had finally made their way across the Jordan River into the promised land of Canaan. Caleb was one of the fearless and faithful men who had been sent, years before, to spy on this land. Now an elderly man in his eighties, he looks away to Mount Hebron and then turns to Joshua, his leader, and says, "Now, therefore, give me this mountain" (Joshua 14:12).

While others chose the ease of the valley, Caleb chose to climb, to conquer the heights, and to use them. The generations that followed him profited by his decision.

When it comes to the way we deal with life's mountains, there are at least three kinds of people. There are the *won'ts*. These look at the mountains and will not try to conquer them. There are the *can'ts*. These try but give up and turn back. Then there are the *cans*. These, like Caleb, say, "Give me this mountain." They see the difficulties ahead, but they know that by God's grace, they will be able to overcome them.

Someone has very well said that although help must come from without, it must be applied within. The One who has given us the vision of the possibilities in life's mountains also gives us the power to claim those mountains. We, however, must apply that power.

Life's experiences may lead us up some rugged mountain trails. But remember, take heart, for so it was with the most noble man that ever lived. This man, Jesus, conquered. By His grace, so may we.

GROWING

There is nothing more exciting than the witnessing of birth and growth. How satisfying it is to see a child grow into a youth. That auntie was wrong when she looked down upon a brand new niece and exclaimed, "Bless its little heart. Wouldn't it be wonderful if she could stay like that?" She was wrong because all life is *meant* to grow.

It was said of the finest young man that ever lived, "And Jesus increased in wisdom and stature, and in favour with God and man" (Luke 2:52).

Growing up involves the developing of muscle and mind. Today we have some of the finest-looking specimens of youth our country has ever known, and they have the greatest opportunity for obtaining knowledge that the world has ever offered. Jesus increased in wisdom and stature and in favor with God and man. The number of years we live has much to do with the number of opportunities we have, but more important is what we do with those opportunities.

It was Jesus who said to two brothers one day, ". . . Come ye after me, and I will make you to become fishers of men" (Mark 1:17). In every avenue of life, we grow as we reach out to others. It is a day-by-day affair.

Recently I heard the story of an aging farmer in West Virginia. He was celebrating his 104th birthday. A reporter from Wheeling was sent to interview him.

"How do you account for your long life?" inquired the reporter.

The farmer replied, "Every morning when I get out of bed, I always say that this is exactly the kind of day I wanted."

The reporter asked, "That's a kind of Pollyanna philosophy, isn't it?"

The alert old gentleman answered, "I don't know this Pollyanna girl, but my philosophy works. I'm here, aren't I?"

A neighbor chimed in with, "Uncle Bill lives each day as

though it was the first day of the rest of his life." Might that not be one of the reasons he had lived so long?

We can live only one day at a time, renewing our faith for each day ahead. As the poet wrote,

> *Do you want to be happy?*
> *I'll tell you the way.*
> *Don't live tomorrow until you've lived today.*
> *So, through prayer and service, live—and grow—one day at a time.*

BEING OBSERVING

The Boy Scouts were going on a hike. Their Scoutmaster asked that each boy be observant and report to him on his return the things he saw.

When the group returned, one boy was asked about what he had observed. He answered, "The same old things that we always see."

But another Scout reported, "The rising sun made the early morning clouds beautiful. There was a mother bird and her young in a tree. She was teaching her little ones to fly. The water in the brook made music as it trickled over the stones."

It seems that we see just about what we are looking for. One night during a storm, two travelers took refuge in a cave. When the storm was over, one of the men looked out and saw nothing but mud. The other man observed how bright the stars were following the storm.

Some housewives see only the drudgery in housekeeping while others discover the joy to be had in making a house a home. Each vocation can be seen as a task that has to be done, or it can be seen as a rewarding way of life.

The Psalm-writer looked out upon a new day. With confidence and joy, he cried out, "This is the day which the Lord hath made; we will rejoice and be glad in it" (Psalm 118:24).

Because this world is inhabited by human beings, it is not perfect. If our minds dwell too much upon the mistakes of yesterday, we will fail to see the wonderful possibilities of the day in which we live.

Recently I stopped to admire a beautiful flower garden. Early this past spring it was a bleak spot crowded with rocks, and the soil was not fertile. But with tender, loving care and the Great Gardener's help, the gardeners had turned the area into a place of beauty that brought words of praise from all who saw it.

It was not so much from whence the disciples of Jesus came as what Jesus saw in them and who he helped them to become. So it is with each of us. Most of us would not be where we are today had someone not observed something worthwhile in us and encourage us.

THE RESPONSIVE CHORD

The thirteen-year-old-boy stood before the judge. He was defiant at every word of the court. Even though he was still in his teens, he had a long record of vandalism and petty law-breaking. This was not the first time the boy had appeared in court.

As the judge was about to sentence him to reform school, he saw a man stand up. Recognizing the man, he asked if there was something he wanted to say.

Joe Emerson, superintendent of a boys' farm, came forward and stood by the lad. "Judge, Your Honor," he said, "I'm not here to condone this boy's acts. I have come forward believing that there is something we can do for him, if you will give me permission."

The judge, knowing Mr. Emerson and his work with young people, looked at the boy. His defiant attitude was gone, and there were tears in his eyes. The superintendent had struck a responsive chord in the youngster.

The judge placed the boy under the jurisdiction of Mr. Emerson. With his firm but kindly guidance and the help of the boys' farm staff, the teenager grew to be a responsible young man. His entire future was changed simply because someone had touched a responsive chord in his life.

How many times incidents like this have been repeated down through the years. It proves that the saying is true: "It is better to mold youth than to reform men."

A woman was brought to Jesus one day. She had been taken in the act of adultry, and according to the law of Moses, she was to be stoned to death. Jesus suggested to her accusers that he who was without sin should cast the first stone. One by one her accusers dropped their stones and went their way.

Jesus did not condone her sin. He counseled her to "...go, and sin no more" (John 8:11). Jesus touched a responsive chord in this woman's life, and her future was changed for the good.

The challenge to Christianity-in-action calls for charity— the granting of another opportunity to one in distress. With this attitude, first exemplified by Jesus, we can often touch the chord that helps to bring harmony out of discord and a future worth living.

THE MARK OF A WINNER

I recently spoke in a church where a sixteen-year-old girl played a piano solo. The title of the solo was "Hail to the Victor." From beginning to end, she held the attention of her audience. One could almost see the Israelites marching around Jericho with Joshua in the lead.

After the service, I asked this young, vivacious, and talented girl how long she had been taking piano lessons. Her answer was, "Forever, for as long as I can remember." This girl had the mark of a winner.

When we read the Faith Chapter, Hebrews 11, we are reminded of those who had the mark of a winner. One who stands out in my mind is Moses. He reckoned that to suffer scorn for the sake of God's people was worth far more than all the treasures of Egypt. Because he kept his eye on the future reward, he had the mark of a winner.

First of all, a winner does not quit. Some have claimed that Moses ran away. True, at one time he did. He was only human. So did Peter deny his Lord. But we cannot run from God, for God always knows where we are and what He needs of us. God found Moses and proved to him, there beside the burning bush, that with His help, Moses could be a winner.

Job cried out in his weakness, "Though he slay me, yet will I trust in him..." (Job 13:15). A winner never quits; a quitter never wins.

Second, a winner is a dreamer. Nothing worthwhile has ever been accomplished without someone having first dreamed about it. A world in which people everywhere would love one another—even their enemies—was the dream of Jesus. It was more than a dream; it was His mission. He proved that it was possible. The world is a far better place because of those who have been inspired by that dream and have given themselves to it.

Last, but not least, a winner sees beyond the present goal. Moses won because he kept his eye on the future. It is not what my winning does for me alone that counts, but what it does for those who come after me.

One evening we watched and listened to the Billy Graham Crusade telecast from Poland. I was inspired by Myrtle Hall's singing of "Amazing Grace." As she sang, I thought that here is a woman singing a song that was written by John Newton, who, before the grace of God changed his life, was the captain of a slave ship that may have transported some of Myrtle Hall's ancestors to this country in its hold.

It is not only the present-day rewards that we think of when we think of winning but those of eternity as well. Today's achievements are the treasures that we lay up in the heaven of which Jesus spoke. They are the rewards of the winner.

WHAT IS IN YOUR HAND?

"Just a handful of individual letters, twenty-six of them. They are called the alphabet," explained our teacher that day long ago in grade school. She went on to say, "With these letters you spell your name. These were all the letters needed to write the Gettysburg Address, the Ten Commandments, and the Constitution of the United States. These are all the letters you will need to spell success or failure."

How insignificant that handful of letters looked to us as our wise teacher spread them out on her desk. As years have come and gone, I have learned how important an indispensable those letters really are. Our lives depend on how we use them.

The farmer holds in his hand some grains of seed, yet in that handful of see lies a potential miracle. What happens in the future depends on whether one sows the seed in the soil or drops it back in the seed bag.

When God needed an agent to lead the Hebrews from the slave-labor camps of Egypt and to mold them into the nation of Israel, He chose a young Hebrew by the name of Moses. It was one thing to choose Moses but another to convince him to act. In the midst of the excuses Moses was making, "... the Lord said unto him, What is that in thine hand? And he said, A Rod" (Exodus 4:2). At the Lord's bidding, Moses dropped the rod on the ground, and it became a serpent. As he reached down to pick it up, it became a rod again.

The rod in itself was not important, except that it was a symbol of what God could do through Moses if only Moses had the courage and the faith to use his resourcefulness on behalf of God and His people.

What is that in your hand? Not much? Just a cup of cold water, a kind word, a sincere smile, a sympathetic tear, a friendly visit, a little bit from our plenty to share with those who have so little, or a song to sing when someone else is sad. Just a cup of cold water, but Jesus said, "... Whosoever shall give you a cup of water to drink in my name, because ye belong to Christ, verily I say unto you, he shall not lose his reward" (Mark 9:41).

James A. Garfield, twentieth president of the United States, experienced many hardships as a youth. But he never gave up. One day he said, "I cannot do everything, but I will not let what I cannot do interfere with what I can do."

Most of us will never become famous in the eyes of the world. It is not important that we become famous, but it is important that we remain faithful. We will never be held responsible for not using a talent we do not possess. It is what we have in our hands and what we do or refuse to do with it that makes the difference. God needs us to complete His plan for us and His creation.

PURSUING PERFECTION

Someone asked Paderswski, the famous Polish pianist who began playing the piano at age of three, "What does it take to become a superb pianist like you?" Paderewski replied, "Practice, practice—ten to to sixteen hours each day."

We have long believed that practice makes perfect. This is the rule we follow in pursuing perfection. Progress is the building on the achievement of yesterday. Our goals should always exceed our reach. These statements are true in all avenues of life.

One of the foremost questions John Wesley, English preacher and founder of the Methodist Church, used to ask young men entering the ministry was, "Are you going on to perfection?" Wesley sought nothing less than the highest for those who would become the spiritual leaders of the church.

To be as good as my neighbor might not always be good

enough. To see our imperfections and try, with God's help, to change them is the attitude of those who seek to grow and develop in spirit.

In His Sermon on the Mount, Jesus gave us the formula for happiness. Some of His most of familiar words are, "Blessed are the pure in heart: for they shall see God" (Matthew 5:8). We become like that with which we associate. If we pray and strive for a perfect heart, we come to see God; we can *feel* His Presence here beside us.

Recently, in the company of a group of farmers whom I had just addressed, someone observed, "It seems to me that farming is a gamble." A young farmer spoke up. "To me, farming is not a gamble; it is a way of life." That young farmer, although he was facing many problems, felt that farming is not only a way of making a living, it's a way of making a life."

The Christian life also has its problems, but it is not a gamble; it is a way of life. To reach the highest goal, we must steadfastly pursue faith in Jesus, Whose life was perfection.

JULY

Freedom's Cost

THE SEEDS OF FREEDOM

Sometime back, while visiting the *Mayflower II* at Plymouth, Massachusetts, we were told of the bare necessities that our Puritan forefathers were permitted to bring along to the New World. On the list were seeds from their native land.

Although those seeds were fragile, they were potent. With them, those determined men and women blazed a trail and established a new nation—a nation that was to eventually form, accept, and defend our Declaration of Independence.

At times it is well that we pause and meditate upon our assets as American citizens. In so doing, we see that we have cause to be grateful for those seeds of freedom that have brought such a great harvest to so many.

What were some of those seeds that our forefathers had with them when they landed at Plymouth Rock? One of them was *vision*. The vision was of a new land of freedom of choice and worship. We can well be grateful for their vision. But without others who followed them, those who too had vision, our country would not have lived to celebrate its 200th Anniversary in 1976.

There were also the seeds of *courage*. Life in the past had not been easy for those settlers. It would be less so in a strange and uncertain land. Only the courageous and determined would survive.

When Moses, the leader of the Israelites in their flight from Egypt, was about to be taken from his people, he encouraged them with the words, "And the Lord, he it is that doth go before thee: he will be with thee, he will not fail thee, neither forsake thee: fear not, neither be dismayed" (Deuteronomy 31:8).

It was with this kind of courage that our nation was established. Why such courage? Mainly because our forebears brought with them a generous supply of the seeds of *faith*.

It was their courageous faith in God that had led them thus far. They knew that He would not forsake them now. Those pilgrims of 1620 were like those who, long before them, crosssed the Jordan to enter a strange land. They were like Abraham and his family, "who went out not knowing whither they went." They remembered that long ago God had said, "I will never leave thee nor forsake thee."

When the present is discouraging and you cannot turn back, when the future looks dark and uncertain, look up. The God of eternity, of which we are a part, will not fail us.

We must continue to show and nurture the seeds of vision, courage, and faith. From these came the sturdy roots of freedom in the past. They can be depended upon for our victories in the future.

VIGILANCE

"In the name of God, Amen." Those are the closing words of the Mayflower Compact, written and signed by those courageous settlers of the New World even before they left the boat. William Bradford, fatherly governor, later called this compact "the birth certificate of American democracy."

Two hundred years have come and gone, and today we are well into the beginning of our third century as American citizens. What this third century has in store for us, only God knows.

It is certain that the words of Josiah Holland, an American historian and poet, are as true today as when he wrote them:

*God give us men.
A time like this demands
Strong minds, great hearts, true faith and ready hands,
Men whom the lust of office does not kill,
Men whom the spoils of office cannot buy,
Men who possess opinions and a will,
Men who have honor, men who will not lie,
Tall men, suncrowned, who live above the fog. . . .*

From the time of Moses until the present, a key word has been *vigilance*. Paul, writing to the Christians at Corinth, knew the importance of the spirit of vigilance when he said, "Watch ye, stand fast in the faith, quit you like man, be strong" (I Corinthians 16:13). Jesus urged His followers to "Watch and pray, that ye enter not into temptation: the spirit indeed is willing, but the flesh is weak" (Matthew 26:41). Watch, be alert; never lower the flag of faith. A quitter never wins; a winner never quits. Be strong, as our forefathers were.

Ten-year-old Jack Bixler was struck by a car in front of his home. His mother was soon at his side. As they waited for the ambulance, Jack looked up at his mother and asked, "Mother, are you frightened?" His mother, with a reassuring smile, answered, "No, son, I'm not frightened." Jack bravely said "Then I won't be either." Jack's courage did not come from trying to be brave. He caught it from someone else.

Courage in the face of danger has been a watchword of the human race from the beginning of time. It has made determined nations even stronger and has helped to save the church from defeat and decay.

"If God be for us, who can be against us?" Paul wrote. With God, one watchful, courageous, faithful person is a majority.

So now, my friend, let us quit ourselves like men. Let us be strong. There is a burden to bear; there is a grief to share; there is a heart that breaks 'neath a load of cars. Go forth with a song. "In the name of God, Amen."

"OF THEE I SING"

Congressman John Warren, who headed the Bicentennial Committee back in 1976, proclaimed, "We are laying a cornerstone for a third century." We are now well into that third century, and it behooves us at this season of the year to recall the foundation upon which we laid that cornerstone.

Very few democracies have endured as long as has our beloved nation. It is well to remember that our democracy was built upon a sound foundation.

When Samuel F. Smith, eminent nineteenth-century clergyman, was a young college student, he was inspired and wrote, within half an hour, a poem he called "America." He began that poem with:

> *My country, tis of thee*
> *Sweet land of liberty*
> *Of thee I sing*

I need scarcely say that those words are the beginning of our best-loved patriotic hymn, beloved by all from its introduction in 1832 to the present day. The song spoke the sentiments of those who were helping to lay the foundation of a nation dedicated to the freedom and opportunity of all those within its borders.

We are prone to look back and to be thankful for our national heritage, and well we should. This nation "under God" came into being and prospered through blood, sweat, and tears, as well as with wise dedication and spiritual emphasis.

We are endeavoring to build upon the foundation of the past. As we do so, we must remember that the cornerstone of this century contains not only the names, exploits, and victories of the past but the hopes, prayers, and dedication of we who live, love, and share in this present day.

The Psalm-writer speaks words of wisdom and hope when he says, "Blessed is the nation whose God is the Lord; and the people whom he hath chosen for his own inheritance" (Psalm 33:12).

The founding and establishment of this our beloved nation was not by accident. History has proven that God's plan was for a new nation to be founded. It was not accomplished, nor has the country continued to grow, without mistakes and sins for which we have had to ask forgiveness.

It is well at this time, when our thoughts turn back to the signing of the Declaration of Independence, for us to bow our heads and pray:

Our Father's God, to Thee,
Author of Liberty,
To Thee we sing.
Long may our land be bright
With freedom's holy light.
Protect us by Thy might,
Great God, our King.

OUR WANTS AND OUR NEEDS

There was a slogan during World War II that said, "Use it up, wear it out. Make it do, or go without." We are often confused in differentiating between our wants and our needs.

The best-loved and most-familiar Psalm begins with, "The Lord is my shepherd; I shall not want" (Psalm 23:1). To me, the Psalm-writer is saying that the Good Shepherd will supply our wants according to our needs.

As we grow older, certain of our wants are not as great as they were when we were rearing our families. Uncle Orlo, my good neighbor of long ago, once said, "God not only supplies our needs, He does so with a bonus. He not only gave us the beautiful rose, He added the perfume."

Luke, the Gospel-writer, has recorded the parable of the Prodigel Son as told by Jesus. This son felt that his wants would never be met at home as they would be if he were out on his own. His greatest wish seem to be for freedom from discipline.

After the father had given this son "his share," the young man went out into the world to get what he wanted. Away from the wise counsel and discipline of his father, he wasted his possessions, and ". . . he began to be in went" (Luke 15:14).

It was Henry Wadsworth Longfellow who wrote, "Most people would succeed in small things if they were not troubled with great ambitions." Ambition is good as long as it does not cause us to confuse our needs with our wants.

Our economy in America is based on a policy of plenty. Plenty of food, plenty of money, plenty of work, and plenty of opportunities. This is one reason why a recession is especially painful.

". . . I shall not want (Psalm 23:1). These are the words of a true believer who had learned to trust God and come to know that the Lord helps those who help themselves.

There is an old Gospel song written by Charles D. Martin that we have been singing for many years. One verse says:

All you may need
He will supply.
Nothing you ask will be denied.
God will take care of you.

ANNIVERSARIES

We too often recount our anniversaries by the tragedies of the past rather than by the happy occasions. We are likely to lament, "That was the year when I broke my leg," or, "That was the winter of the big blizzard." Why not say, "That was the year when our entire family got through the winter without coming down with the flu?"

While there are some anniversaries that all of us would like to forget, there are many others to which we look back with thanksgiving.

On July 25, 1925, Thelma and I said "I do" to one another. In those early years we experienced some rough times, but love has a way of helping two people who love each other and who take God into their partnership. The rich experiences have far outweighed the poor, and are indeed wealthier for them.

A wedding takes only ten minutes; a marriage takes a lifetime. A happy marriage is not one wherein two people learn to always think alike but one in which they learn to think *together*.

I have often said that Thelma has been a wonderful homemaker, companion, and mother. She has been a good listener too, not that she hasn't had her say! She has had the same "preacher" for almost sixty years, yet she continues to offer me encouragement and cheer.

Paul was aware of the importance of the mutual relationship of husband and wife. He wrote, "Husbands, love your wives, even as Christ also loved the Church, and gave himself for it . . ." (Exphsians 5:25).

There is no other ingredient that makes the years richer than that of love—the kind of love that does not ask, but gives instintingly. Whether it be the first marriage anniversary or the sixtieth, love is the lubricant that makes the machinery of marriage run smoothly.

The most important thing is not how much a couple accumulates in the bank but how much and how well they have learned to invest together in those things of the heart that will last throughout the years.

These are the anniversaries that make one look back in nostalgic memory and forward with hope. These are the times that cause us to bow our heads in humble gratitude to Him Who has led us and kept us.

THE TEST OF UNITY

Recently a devoted and lovable couple celebrated their sixty-fifth wedding anniversary. Someone asked the husband what he thought the secret was of their long and happy married life. The silver-haired man replied with a twinkle in his eye, "Many things, but one thing for certain. We learned to agree to disagree without becoming disagreeable." He then concluded with, "But mainly we pledged to share together in all things, and that covers a lot ot territory."

I have been thinking of this goodman's words. Thelma and I still have a way to go before we will celebrate sixty-five years of married life. We too have learned to share together in all things. She has been a good housekeeper, but—more than that—a good homekeeper. We have shared the good days and the bad, the happy with the sad.

This kind of sharing should be true not only in marriage but in all of life. Harmony and togetherness go hand in hand. Our application of them spells the difference between victory and defeat in our relationships with one another.

Harmony is realized by first obtaining the true pitch and then keeping in tune. A teacher of the violin once said that it takes much disciplined practice to become a good violinist. He was right. Harmony in life, as in marriage or music, demands our undivided attention.

The Psalm-writer said, "Behold, how good and how pleasant it is for brethren to dwell together in unity!" (Psalm 133:1). Brotherly love has been the hope and prayer of man from the beginning of time. Men have even died for it. Real unity, however, demands not only that we be willing to die for it but that we also be willing to live for it. The power to do so comes from without, but it must be applied within.

The apostle Paul gave us true words of wisdom when he wrote, "Though I speak with the tongues of men and of angels, and have not charity [love], I am become as sounding brass, or a tinkling cymbal" (I Corinthians 13:1).

Harmony, or unity, will not come to the world only through the tongues of men; love from the heart and deeds of mercy are required of us too. Jesus exemplified the truth. It was later restated by one of His disciples, John, when he wrote, "... let us not love in word, neither in tongue; but in deed and in truth" (I John 3:18).

The true reward of unity, out in the world as well as in the home, rests upon our decision to put actions above words. Jesus gave us the formula. With His help, we can apply it.

TIME OUT

Corn planting was finished. The garden was plowed and planted, and the first cutting of hay was in the barn. The wheat was beginning to head. There is never a dull moment on the farm, but there is a time every now and then to catch your breath and take a little rest. This, then, was when we dug some worms and took out the fishing poles. The occasion called for indulging oneself with a little lazy spell along the river.

Occasions like that were always good opportunities for relaxation and for refreshing oneself for the busy times ahead. A wise man once observed that no time is ever lost while we take time out to study our direction and to check our goals.

When we take time out for a retreat today, we will be in less danger of retreating tomorrow.

One of the greatest leaders in Old Testament days was Moses. He was not perfect in his decisions—for he was human. When he fled from Egypt to Midian and was in the mountains caring for his father-in-law's sheep, he witnessed a miracle. Most of us remember the story of the burning bush. When Moses saw this bush, which was not being consumed but continued to burn, he stopped to watch it—and this is exactly what the Lord wanted him to do. When God has a task for us, He first of all gets our attention. So Moses took time out to watch the burning bush. As he did so, God spoke to him and convinced him that He made a mission for him.

Even Jesus found it necessary to take time out to slip away for rest and prayer. He once said to His disciples, "... Come ye yourselves apart into a desert place, and rest a while..." (Mark 6:31). These followers of their Master needed those moments of refreshment with Him, a withdrawl from the pressures all about them.

A friend of mine tells me that a camping trip for the entire family provides more than mere relaxation. "One of the most important things," he says, "is getting the entire family together in one place, away from the hurry of the world, where we can talk about making a life as well as a living."

Taking time out is not only refreshing but oftentimes most fruitful. Taking time out to visit a shut-in is time well spent. Time out to write that letter we have been neglecting gives satisfaction to the writer as well as to the receiver. Taking time out to read and study the Bible as well as to thank God for His many blessings brings profound refreshment to the soul. In doing these things, they become a part of our daily routine of living, as they should be.

PEACEMAKING

"We seek peace, an enduring peace..." President Franklin D. Roosevelt wrote. These were some of the last words of an address he expected to make in the next few days at the organizational meeting of the United Nations at San Francisco. He did not have the opportunity to make that address for he died, suddenly, on the day following the writing of his speech. But his words express the longing of people everywhere.

Peace is a gift from God to those who submit to the formula for peace. "Blessed are the peacemakers: for they shall be called the children of God" (Matthew 5:9), Jesus counseled in His memorable Sermon on the Mount. This informs us that peace is something that has to be *won*.

I learned my first lesson in making a flower bed from my mother, who loved her garden. I learned that one first prepares the soil, then sows the seed or sets out the plants. I soon found that one has to care for the tender plants or the weeds will take over. Making peace is much like making a flower bed—they both call for eternal vigilance.

What are some of the ingredients of peace? *Love* belongs to peace. Jesus taught that one could not have real peace of mind as long as he harbored ill will against anyone, even against his enemies. He said, "... Love your enemies ... pray for them which despitefully use you, and persecute you ..." (Matthew 5:44).

Forgiveness belongs to peace. Peace is found only in the hearts of those who have learned to forgive and forget.

Faith is another ingredient of peace. It is not easy to have faith in someone who has wronged us. The great Master Peacemaker said to His disciples before He left them, "These things have I spoken unto you, that in me you might have peace" (John 16:33).

Joan Green was in a state of turmoil and far from home. One day in an unfamiliar church she listened to a sincere pastor say, "Peace may not mean release from every irritation. Often happiness and hardship go together." On that very day Joan discovered the peace that "passeth all understanding." "I found a peace that I never knew could be mine," she wrote. "I still have some problems now and then that have to be solved, but I have Someone to help me solve them," she concluded. Joan

Green went on to become a most capable and understanding nurse. In her daily work she has led many others to find the same peace that has helped her.

There is nothing that gives serenity to our minds and lends us confidence for the future like the peace that comes from complete submission to God and His will for us.

AUGUST

Keys to Successful Living

HOW TO FACE DISCOURAGEMENT

"What is this world coming to?" The spokesman was a man who had experienced many problems during the past year. Another member of our informal group responded with, "George, might it not be better to say, "Look what has come to this world?" Then she pointed to the many opportunities open to those who live by their faith in the present and their hopes for the future.

How should we face discouragement? Our way is not to dwell on what the future may hold but on He Who holds the future. The power of God within us is greater than any evil power around us.

We become despondent when we dwell upon what is wrong with the world. Might it not be better for us to be thankful for what is right in the world? True, there was never a time in our memory when the crime rates were higher, the morale lower, and human life cheaper. But on the other hand, we still have the spirit of sharing and our freedom of speech. We still have open church doors. We have a society concerned for the future of its young people and for the care of its aged.

If we become discouraged by all the sin we see about us, we should also be encouraged by all the grace and mercy that abound.

Many years ago a captain of a slave boat delivered his cargo to London. As he left the ship, half drunk, he passed a little mission. Hearing music, he went in. The music and the sermon touched him, and God's grace served him. That young man, John Newton, later wrote,

> *Amazing grace*
> *how sweet the sound*
> *That saved a wretch like me.*

Either we walk in the light of faith or we stand in the shadow of doubt. Paul tells us, "We are troubled on every side, yet not distressed . . . Persecuted, but not forsaken, cast down, but not destroyed" (II Corinthians 4:8-9).

Horatio Spafford was a Chicago businessman. At the time of the great Chicago fire in 1871 he lost all but his wife and children. He decided to send them back to England until he could get things under control. There was a shipwreck. Mrs. Spafford was saved, but the two children were lost. From England, Mrs. Spafford cabled her husband, "Saved—but alone."

In despair but with faith, Horatio Spafford later wrote,

> *When peace like a river, attendeth my way,*
> *When sorrows like sea billows roll,*
> *Whatever my lot*
> *Thou hast taught me to say*
> *It is well, it is well with my soul.*

This man had learned how to face sorrow and discouragement. By God's help, so may we.

PLAYING THE RESTS

"Rest is not a sedative for the sick but a tonic for the strong." I once read these words on a well-lit bulletin board. To me, they pointed to a fact that we often ignore: There is dignity not only in honest labor but in well-earned rest.

It reminds me of a neighbor who used to come out to the farm to work for my father. Tamer Mason was a good workman, but he could also "take a break" and sit in the shade, where he would be asleep in just a few moments.

He said one day, "When I work, I work hard. When I rest, I sit loose." Many of us have learned to work hard but have failed to learn the benefits of "sitting loose."

David described the secret of resting when he wrote Psalm 37, especially when he said, "Rest in the Lord, and wait patiently for him. . ." (Psalm 37:7).

A favorite music teacher of mine used to say, "When you practice your music, be sure and play the rests. They are a part of the music, you know." Playing the rests means to *pay attention* to the rests. Never pass them by. There is dignity in labor, but there is also a deep necessity for rest. It is the pause that often develops some of our best ideas.

Jesus even urged His disciples to ". . . Come ye yourselves apart into a desert place, and rest a while . . ." (Mark 6:31).

At this season of the year when we pause to pay honor to honest labor, we remember that Jesus emphasized the dignity of labor and that He Himself was a carpenter. He also taught that we should not only be worthy of our hire but also deserving of our rest.

Rest in the Lord. . . . Commit to Him your labors, your hopes, and your leisure. This is what real life is all about.

THE KEY TO HAPPINESS

A letter from one of the readers of a column I write asked, "Would you please write something that I can give to my best friend, who has plenty to live *on* but so very little, it seems, to live *for*."

A little booklet, *How Can We Be Truly Happy?* was born in answer to that letter. It is impossible in the space of four hundred words for me to write all that is contained in that little booklet. The following, however, is a resume of its contents.

First, to be truly happy, one must learn to live one day at a time. This takes courage, faith, and hope. You can think of this day as the last day of your life or look at it as the first day of the rest of your life. Despair is the attitude of the first, faith the outlook of the second.

Second, live not alone for yourself but for others. It was Paul who wrote, "Bear ye one another's burdens, and so fulfill the law of Christ" (Galatians 6:2). Our burdens are made lighter and our lives happier by sharing our troubles with each other.

The third step to the key of happiness is to be aware of the true source of life. Every living thing has a source from whence it received its birth and existence. Jesus told us, "I am the light of the world: he that followeth me shall not walk in darkness . . ." (John 8:12).

This leads me to say that if we are to be truly happy, we must maintain the discipline of prayer. When the battles of life bring discouragement, when you are almost overcome by strife, look up—have faith. God cares. Don't faint, but pray.

One of the reasons why so many of us have almost fainted by the wayside is that it took us so long to learn to pray the most difficult prayer of all—the prayer of relinquishment, when we find ourselves letting go and letting God.

Last, but not least, to be truly happy, one must learn the secret of a life lived in love. Love is the lubricant that keeps the machinery of life running smoothly. Sincere love helps us to understand the faults of others and appreciate their virtues.

To be truly happy, we must keep faith and hope alive— but *love* is the anchor that holds life steady. Love is the greatest power of all, for God is love. Only when love is the dominant force in our lives will we be truly happy.

OBEDIENCE

"What beautiful eyes. . . . and just look at the character in those ears." The subject of the comments was handsome-looking German shepherd seeing-eye dog. The light changed to green, and we started across the street together. The dog stayed close to its master, who was blind, and each was trusting the other.

As I witnessed the incident, I was reminded of another. One evening I listened to a trainer of seeing-eye dogs as he explained the training procedure. After telling us of the kind of dogs that were chosen and describing some of their characteristics, he said, "The first thing the dog must learn is obedience."

The first law of any worthy endeavor is obedience. A wise man of many years observed, "We shall never be masters of others until we have learned to be mastered."

During the first years of Jesus' life, He knew obedience. When He was twelve years old, His parents found Him in the temple at Jerusalem. He went back home with them to Nazareth, ". . . and was subject unto them. . . " (Luke 2:51). When later in His life Jesus was led up into the wilderness of temptation, He proved to Satan that He was mastered by a far greater power than evil could ever muster.

Our Master's whole life was the way of obedience. In the garden of Gethsemane, where He prayed on the night before His death, He was able to say, ". . . nevertheless, not my will, but thine, be done" (Luke 22:42).

Paul learned obedience while traveling the road to Damascus. There, in his blindness, he cried out, ". . . Lord, what wilt thou have me to do?" (Acts 9:6).

George Fox, the stalwart Quaker Christian of another generation, once said, "A strong will is good; it all depends on whose will it is."

There is a wonderful old Gospel hymn that we all still love to sing. It was written by John H. Sammis, a faithful pastor and writer of his day. Mr. Sammis said that the words came to him when he was experiencing a deep sorrow. The first verse of the song says:

> When we walk with the Lord
> In the light of His word,
> What a glory He sheds on our way.
> When we do His good will,
> He abides with us still
> And with all who will trust and obey.

Yes, only by a willing obedience to God can we have peace of mind and joyous living.

KEEPING HOPE ALIVE

A recent letter from one of the readers of my column, "Sermonettes," began: "Your sermonettes are not masterpieces. They are not composed of high-sounding phrases and words that one cannot pronounce. But, may I say, each sermonette inspires hope."

I was grateful for that letter, and especially for the last sentence. It caused me to take inventory and to ask myself, "Am I an inspirer of hope?"

In our daily living, do we suggest despair, or do we inspire hope? Hope is like faith. When hope is gone, there is nothing left. Hope is the foundation of the present and trust in the outcome of the future. In all things it is better to hope than to despair. When there is no hope, there is no dream.

Away back in the Old Testament there is buried a little book of only four chapters. While it is a book that contains moments of despair, its main character is an inspiration of hope. It is the Book of Ruth.

Naomi had come to Moab with her husband and her two sons, only to lose all three of them through death. She found herself far from her homeland with only her two daughters-in-law for comfort. She decided it best that she return to her native country and her kinsman. But she advised her daughters-in-law to remain in Moab, where their future would be more promising.

One of the warmest and most moving phrases in the entire Old Testament is the response of Ruth to her mother-in-law: "... Intreat me not to leave thee, or to return from following after thee: for whither thou goest, I will go; and where thou lodgest, I will lodge: thy people shall be my people, and thy God my God" (Ruth 1:16).

Hope is the song of the first early morning bird while the world is yet dark. Ruth sang that song of hope. Ruth's words of dedication and love helped to change the lament of Naomi to a song of hope.

Hope is the song that gives harmony to life's goals. Hope is the light that burns brighter with the years. Hope is eternal. It shines steadily from one generation to another. It did so for the generations that followed Ruth. Hope is worth striving for.

Joaquin Miller, an American poet, read the words that day after day Columbus had written in the log of his first voyage across the unchanted Atlantic: "This day we sailed on." Storms had ravaged the ships, the *Pinta* had lost her rudder, and the men were threatening mutiny. As Joaquin Miller read those words, he began to write. In the poem he called "Columbus," we find the lines,

> *What shall we do when hope is gone?*
> *The words leapt like a leaping sword:*
> *"Sail on! Sail on! Sail on!"*

This is the kind of courage that hope through Christ gives each of us.

THE WELL IS DEEP

Life's wells can be shallow or deep—it all depends on our choice. Fortunate is the person who, in times of his greatest thirst and need, has chosen the deep wells and has found something with which to draw its waters.

One day Jesus was resting at Jacob's well. A woman of Samaria came there, as was her custom, to draw water. She was surprised that Jesus would converse with her, she being a Samaritan. He even went so far as to ask her for a drink of water and then told her that if she knew who He was and had asked Him for water, He would have given her "living water."

"The woman saith unto him, Sir, thou hast nothing to draw with, and the well is deep: from whence then hast thou that living water?" (John 4:11). She spoke the language she knew. She was talking about the impossible.

First of all, to draw from the deep wells of life, one must have a faith that is alive. This does not mean that we understand all of the mysteries but that we are willing to reach out in faith. The lasting resources are not to be found on the surface of life; they are to be found in the depths.

To reach this water that quenches our thirst, we must also admit that the well is deep and that we must have something with which to draw forth the water.

Of this woman at the well we might say:

She came to the well to quench her thirst.
'Twas a daily trip for her.
She paused to talk with the Master first.
Odd questions did there occur.
The well was deep, she did confess.
Her well was shallow and full of stress
New hope and light came to her that day
As she left her water pot and hurried away.

We reach the source of this spiritual living water through an habitual prayer life. The well is deep. Jesus Himself found that He needed something with which to draw. Oftentimes He slipped away to the mountains to pray. Each of us needs a mountain also, a place where we may go to pray.

Yes, life's wells can be shallow or deep—the choice is up to us.

CHOOSING THE TIME

There is a time and a place for all things. Most of us have heard those words for as long as we can remember. A wise man of long ago may have said them first when he wrote, "To every thing there is a season, and a time to every purpose under the heaven . . ." (Ecclesiastes 3:1).

This man of wisdom uses the first eight verses of Chapter 3 in Ecclesiastes to tell us that there is "a time" for all things. God has given us the power of choice, and our decisions may not always be wise. Making the wise choice and seeing it through takes the help of a wisdom far greater than our own.

Due to space and time, I mention here only two of the axioms of the writer of Ecclesiastes. First he says that there is "a time to weep." There are many kinds of tears. There are tears of pain, sorrow, remorse, and even tears of joy. Each kind can bring blessed relief.

Henry Werd Beecher, a famous and saintly pastor of another generation, observed that "tears and the telescope through which we see far into Heaven.

How true those words are! If we could not weep, our hearts would break. Tears are the relief valves of the soul. Jesus taught that "Blessed are they that mourn: for they shall be comforted" (Matthew 5:4). Comfort comes only as we mourn and are sorry for our sins and mistakes.

But our lives are not meant to be spent in weeping. There is also "a time to laugh" (Ecclesiastes 3:4). After the storm comes the rainbow. A Christian should be a happy person.

My good neighbor Uncle Orlo had a saying, "A religion that makes one look sick cannot be expected to heal the world." The example set by his life was that of the joy of happy, wholesome living.

I recently ran across a little card on which were the words, "Laughter is God's hand on the shoulder of a troubled world." I long ago observed that a beautiful smile on the countenance is as the sunbeam on the land—they both change drabness into beauty. A smile is truly the whisper of the laugh. It was Mark Twain who said, "Wrinkles should merely indicate where smiles have been."

There is a time for all things, but choice determines the outcome. For many years my daily prayer has been, "Lord, I will utterly fail without Thee; with Thee, I cannot fail." There is a time for all things, and there certainly is a time to pray for guidance.

LIVING LIFE AT ITS BEST

"Hope for the best; prepare for the worst; take what comes with a smile and thanksgiving." Those were the words that I wrote many years ago in an autograph book handed to me by a newly married couple.

In less than two years this fine couple was in an automobile accident, caused by a driver who failed to observe a stop sign. Shannon, the husband, died within a few hours. Ester was spared. Recently she told me, with a smile of courage and faith, that after all these years, she is still trying, by God's help, to hope for the best, to prepare for the worst, and to take what comes with a smile and thanksgiving.

Living life at its best—at any age—means living it with hope. The life and times of a man by the name of Abraham give us the stimulating and challenging story of a brave man of Ur. The Bible tells us that "By faith Abraham, when he was called to go out into a place which he should after receive for an inheritance, obeyed; and he went out, not knowing whither he went" (Hebrews 11:8). Abraham was a pilgram and a wanderer, but a wanderer with purposes and hope. Without hope, we are only half alive. With hope in God, all things are possible.

If we are to live life at its best, we must prepare for whatever may come, good or bad. Prepare for the worst. Most of us have found that at times trouble will come and that the burdens are more than we can bear alone. Many of us have discovered that with God's ever-present aid, we can make bridges of our burdens.

My good friend Uncle Orlo once said to me at a time when I needed his words of comfort, "Life entails sacrifice, suffering, and tears, but God has promised never to leave us nor forsake us." I have found from experience that he was right. Again, in living life at its best, we take what comes with a smile and thanksgiving.

Thelma and I enjoy eating at a certain restaurant in our town for two reasons. The food is good, and the waitress is cheerful and efficient. We always try to sit in a certain section where we will be served by the same waitress, who is special to us. She serves us with a warmth and a smile, and I am sure that her tips must reflect the appreicative feelings of others also.

It is said that a cheerful countenance brightens the day, scatters gloom, and drives the clouds away.

Hoping for the best, preparing for whatever comes—and doing it with a smile and thanksgiving—can better be accomplished when we place our faith in Christ our Lord, Who proved that, with Him, anything is possible. In so doing, not only are we able to live life at its best, but the influence of our lives will encourage others to do likewise.

LIVING VICTORIOUSLY

*Life is what we make it
as we live from day to day,*

Said my good friend Uncle Orlo, many years ago. I replied, "Yes, life is fragile, we should handle it with care."

It was at about the same time in my ministry that I ran across the following formula for living victoriously. It is not new. I first discovered it as a prayer: "Lord, help me to change those things that can be changed. Help me to accept those things that cannot be changed. Lord, give me the wisdom to know the one from the other."

The apostle Paul was so successful after his Damascus-road revelation, he tells us, that he was given a thorn in his flesh lest he be exalted above measure. "For this thing I besought the Lord thrice, that it might depart from me" (II Corinthiens 12:8). Paul might as well have been praying, "Lord, help me to change those things that can be changed."

Even though change is not always advancement, we know that the world is a better place in which to live today because of those individuals who were not satisfied with some of the conditions they saw around them. It is true that life is about what we make it. We live the life we build for ourselves.

There are times in our lives, however, when we discover that we cannot change conditions. Paul experienced this. His prayer then might have been, "Lord, help me to accept those things that cannot be changed."

The answer to his plea for the removal of the thorn in his flesh was, "... My grace is sufficient for thee: for my strength is made perfect in weakness" (II Corinthians 12:9).

Oftentimes the word most difficult to face is *acceptance*. Acceptance is not weakness. It is not giving up. It is giving over to God.

Our victory comes when we pray for the wisdom to know that even though we cannot be rid of certain "thorns in the flesh," we can, by God's grace, live victoriously. We too can say with Paul, "I can do all things through Christ which strengtheneth me" (Philippians 4:13).

SEPTEMBER

How to Find Peace

BE STILL AND KNOW

"Boy, that's power!" A father and his son were sitting in the family car, waiting for the traffic signal to change. As the light changed to green, a motorcycle next to their car took off with a deafening roar. "Dad, that's real power!" exclaimed the eight-year-old son. The father pressed the accelerator of the big Cadillac; it moved smoothly with the traffic.

To some people, noise denotes power. To others, stillness is an illustration of quiet confidence.

A doctor recently said, "Today many young people are losing their hearing from the loud noise they call music."

The Psalm-writer concludes one of his Psalms by saying, "Be still, and know that I am God..." (Psalm 46:10).

Did you ever hear corn growing? I have walked through the shoulder-high corn following a refreshing rain. As the corn drank in the rain and became warmed by the rays of the sun, I seemed to hear it growing in the gentle rustle of its blades in the breeze. That is *power*! The power of nature and her Creator.

There is an interesting incident found in the Chapter 19 of the first Book of Kings. It tells of an experience that affected the life of Elijah, the prophet.

Elijah, who for the safety of his life had taken refuge in a mountain cave, was led to leave the cave and stand on the mountain. As he did so, a destructive wind struck the mountain. This was followed by an earthquake that shook the mountain, followed by a fire. But God was not in the wind, the earthquake, or the fire.

Following the rushing wind, the blasting earthquake, and the blazing fire, there was "a still small voice" (I Kings 19:12). After God had gained the attention of Elijah by proving that He could move the world, He spoke to the prophet in a still small voice.

The world, at times, has cringed with fear of the so-called "power" of harsh dictators. These men conquered for a while, but in the end they went down to defeat.

The man of Galilea exemplifies the greatest power of all—the power of *love*. The followers of Jesus continue to echo the words of Isaiah, who said, ". . . In quietness and in confidence shall be your strength . . ." (Isaiah 30:15).

Be still, my friend whose days seem uncertain, whose burdens are too heavy to bear alone. Let the storms rage. Even in the midst of the worst gale, He says, "Know that I am God." He Who had the first word will have the last.

THE LEAVEN OF LIFE

"Mama baked biscuits for breakfast every morning for forty years," my father used to brag. As I recall, she also prepared and baked yeast bread every week for many years. One of the necessary ingredients in that tasty bread was yeast. Without it, the dough would not rise. The yeast was the leaven.

The leaven of life is important. It can not only enrich and

improve our own lives, it can influence the lives of those around us.

Jesus warned His disciples, "... beware of the leaven of the Pharisees and of the Sacducees" (Matthew 16:6). He also said to them, "Ye are the salt of the earth ..." (Matthew 5:13). Both of those statements concern the leaven of life. We are to beware of the first but to appropriate the second.

The leaven of the Pharisees was hatred, jealousy, and hypocrisy. The leaven of the salt was love, forgiveness, and influence for good. Our influence, for good or for evil, can be the leaven that helps or hinders those with whom we com in contact.

Jesus, when speaking in parables, once observed, "... The kingdom of heaven is like unto leaven, which a woman took, and hid in three measures of meal, till the whole was leavened" (Matthew 13:33).

As a child, I used to be intrigued as I watched the dough rise after my mother had mixed and placed it in a warm place. The leaven worked quietly. I did not understand how it did it. Nor can I explain how kindness and love influence lives for good.

I think of a Sunday School teacher I once knew. He was not only a capable teacher but there was something about him that attracted and held the interest of his class. That class stayed on in the church. Its members became the leaven that continues to keep that church alive today.

The leaven of those first disciples was the Presence of the Holy Spirit. That Presence Jesus promised them if they would tarry, pray, and go. This is the leaven that the world needs today.

ONE DAY AT A TIME

In our human life span there is yesterday, today, and tomorrow. Although it is too late to change or do much about yesterday, we can at least profit by our mistakes and be encouraged by our successes. There is no use to worry about tomorrow and what might happen. It seems that all we have left is today.

I once found the following words: "Tomorrow is a promissory note; Yesterday is a canceled check; Today is the only cash we have left, so spend it wisely."

While visiting with a doctor several years ago, I was somewhat startled when he said, "Well, Reverend, I suppose you are getting people ready to die?" My answer was, "No sir, Doctor, my business is to help people get ready to live, and the dying will take care of itself."

Today is now. That is where we are. This does not mean, however, that we should not prepare for tomorrow. Recently a man came to our table where I was autographing my book, *A Time to Remember*. After leafing through its pages, he said, "I can't dig that. I live for tomorrow and forget yesterday."

Jesus did not condemn those who prepare for tomorrow. He was simply concerned that we not worry or be anxious about it. One version of Matthew 6:34 reads, "Don't be anxious about tomorrow, live one day at a time."

"Whereas ye know not what shall be on the morrow. For what is your life? It is even a vapour, that appeareth for a little while, and then vanisheth away. For that ye ought to say, If the Lord will, we shall live, and do this, or that" (James 4:14-15).

It is important that we keep our dreams alive as long as we live. Our dreams keep us living today with hope for tomorrow.

It was Caleb who, when asked by Joshua what part of the Promised Land he desired for an inheritance, replied, ". . . give me this mountain. . ." (Joshua 14:12). It was said that Caleb was at that time eighty-five years of age. There is something about a dream that makes us forget our age.

We are told to "Boast not thyself of to morrow. . ." (Proverbs 27:1). But we can live today and be thankful for its opportunities, give thanks for the memories of the past, and hope and plan for tomorrow under God's will.

HOPE, OR DESPAIR?

"Quite often man's way is to sink in despair, while God's way is to always rise with hope." These were words often spoken by an English teacher of my youth.

It is true that hope seems to evade us at times, and we see only our present despair.

Recently I visited with a friend, an American citizen of many years. During our visit, this friend said, "I've lost confidence in the government. I don't think I will ever vote again." After listening to his voice of despair, I answered, "I agree that the future does not look good, but we ourselves are to a great extent the government. The future may depend on how we use the privilege of voting. Otherwise this freedom we enjoy could be taken from us."

Paul, in writing to the courageous Christians at Rome, said, "For we are saved by hope . . . But if we hope for that we see not, then do we with patience wait for it" (Romans 8:24-25).

Someone has observed that we are not only to tell it as it is but how it can be. Even though the present may look dark, with hope that future can be different. "Happy is he . . . whose hope is in the Lord his God . . ." (Psalm 146:5), so said the Psalm-writer.

A few weeks ago we visited one of the missions in southern Kentucky. There we saw both hope and despair. Despair at the lack of present and future opportunities for so many of the mountain people. Hope for so many of them who are taking advantage of the opportunities offered them by our mission schools.

A young man of those mountains had run into trouble with the law, and he was brought before the judge at the county seat. The lad's attorney called attention to the fact that this young man was an underprivileged youth of the mountain community.

The judge in the case responded, "I too was one of those underprivileged youths of these mountains, but in spite of it, by

God's help and with the concern of those who cared, I rose from despair to hope."

Man's way is to sink into despair; God's way is to rise with hope.

What tomorrow may bring to our nation, we do not know. What the future hath in store for each of us, we are not sure. But this we do know: If we keep our hope in God alive, we will never be overcome by despair.

LIFE'S INDISPENSABLE INGREDIENT

Recently I listened with interest to an environmentalist speaking on what he said was his favorite subject, "Water—Life's Indispensable Ingredient." He reminded me of some of the things we have known for years but have not taken as seriously as we should.

As I listened, I agreed with him. But as important as water may be to our health, I thought of another indispensable ingredient, equally important to our health.

Peace is surely one of life's indispensable ingredients. We may search the world over, but the ingredient for peace is to be found only within ourselves.

The Old Testament prophet Isaiah said, "Thou wilt keep him in perfect peace, whose mind is stayed on thee: because he trusteth on thee" (Isaiah 26:3).

True peace seems to have evaded so many of us, not because we do not know how to find it but because we are unwilling to pay the price for it.

As I think of this truly significant ingredient of life, I have come to this conclusion: First, peace and greed cannot live in the same heart. This is as true as saying that love and hate cannot dwell together.

Second, peace is not to be found in our possessions but in our gratitudes. Someone has observed that if we have not peace within ourselves, it is vain to seek it from outward sources.

On the final evening before His trial, Jesus was counseling His disciples and said, "Peace I leave with you, my peace I give unto you: not as the world giveth, give I unto you. Let not your heart be troubled, neither let it be afraid" (John 14:27).

These words lead us to believe that we can have peace in the very presence of conflict if we have that Spirit within that helps us to cope with the difficulties of life.

Finally, peace comes to us only as we give it to others. It is like keeping Christmas; we can keep Christmas only by giving it away. A part of the angels' announcement on the hillside that lovely night long ago was, "Glory to God in the highest, and on earth peace, good will toward men" (Luke 2:14).

Is not this the answer? We have peace only as we—acting in the spirit of Christ—show good will to others. We will be the richer for it. The world cannot continue to live without it.

THE FORMULA FOR VICTORIOUS LIVING

"It seems that in every avenue of life I've been a failure," a reader of one of my columns wrote. She continued, "Could you give me a formula for victorious living?"

None of us is without feeling at times that we have failed. This does not mean that we are failures. None of us has all the answers for the perfect life.

Many years ago, however, I discovered that there are at least three ingredients for victorious living. Those ingredients are: thinking, trying, and trusting. I know there are many others, but I suggest these three for now.

A wise teacher of my youth often quoted the words, "You are what you think, if you think about it often enough." I have frequently thought of that bit of wisdom. Think failure, and we will be defeated. Think victory, and it will help us to be victorious. Think illness, and we can make ourselves ill. Think health, and it assists us in healing. The wise man of Proverbs wrote, ". . . as he thinketh in his heart, so is he . . ." (Proverbs 23:7).

Thinking will not make us perfect. However, thinking upon the things that are uplifting will cause us to reach up to Him Who can help us to climb the ladder that leads to the more victorious life.

Again, the present and the future of our lives depend to a great extent on how hard we try to reach our goals. One is a failure only when he or she quits trying.

Quite often some of us are called upon to give an appraisal of a person who is seeking a position. There is one qustion that is usually asked: "Is this person one who loses heart and quits trying when the going is difficult?" Trying encourages our efforts. Truly, the Lord helps those who help themselves.

The third ingredient for victorious living is trust. The farmer loses his crop. Does he give up? No, he keeps sowing—and trusting. It was Paul who learned the secret of victory and wrote, "I can do all things through Christ which strengtheneth me" (Philippians 4:13).

Think of these things: Do not give up trying, and continue to trust in God's promises. This is the road that leads us to victorious living.

THE RIGHT SIDE OF THE BOAT

"What's the matter with him?" I asked my barber as I noticed a man limping down the sidewalk, all humped over.

"Been fishing through the ice for forty years," Frosty replied. "Old Jake Lemmon has been fishing these lakes as long as I can remember." He chuckled, continued to cut my hair, and then concluded with, "Old Jake has always known which side of the boat his bread has been buttered on."

As I watched Old Jake limp on down the street, I little thought that my barber had stated a truth that I would recall forty years later.

I am sure that I have not always known on which side of the boat my bread was buttered. Most of us have found ourselves fishing from the wrong side of the boat at times. We wondered why life had gone stale or why we had lost the joy of living.

Several of the disciples of Jesus had been fisherman before they left their nets to follow Him. It was not strange, then, that following the Resurrection of Jesus, they should, at the invitation of Peter, go fishing.

On this particular occasion of which John tells in his Gospel, they had fished all night without success. When morning came, a voice from the shore inquired if they had caught any fish.

When they replied that they had not, the voice, which was that of Jesus, called out, "... Cast the net on the right side of the ship, and ye shall find" (John 21:6). In so doing, their net filled to overflowing.

Often our answer to a new proposal is, "We never did it that way before," or, "I tried it once, and it failed."

If you are discouraged; if your night has been long and dark; if you have felt like giving up, if you have tried just about every remedy withot success, hear the voice as those men of long ago heard it. "Cast your net on the right side of the boat," and you will find peace and the renewed joy of living. On the right side of the boat you will find forgiveness through prayer, And there, through sharing with others, you will find the abundant life and the peace that will find your "net" to overflowing.

TELLING IT AS IT IS

Recently I received a unique letter. In part it said, "Why don't you tell it as it is? Don't you know that the book you call the Holy Bible is a book of violence, sex, and murder?"

I was sorry that the letter was unsigned. I would like to have answered it, saying, "Yes, I know there are episodes of murder, sex, and violence in our Holy Bible. They had to tell it like it was. But if we too tell it like it is, we must also say that the Bible is a Book of justice, mercy, and love. Just as the Bible tells of a power that would tempt us to sin, so it also tells us of a Power that helps us to overcome evil and temptation."

The Holy Bible tells it as it is. It points out that there are two ways: the way of life, and the way of death. The wise writer of Proverbs said, "There is a way that seemeth right unto a man, but the end thereof are the ways of death" (Proverbs 16:25). The apostle Paul, having experienced both ways of life writes, "Be not deceived; God is not mocked: for whatsoever a man soweth, that shall he also reap" (Galatians 6:7). Paul goes on to point out two ways of sowing: the sowing to the flesh, and the sowing to the Spirit. He tells it as it is. The Bible is that kind of Book.

It is sad, but it is true—the life of David, the Psalm-writer, was not without the blemish of sin. It was only as the merciful hand of God touched him after his confession of sin that he became the man who was able to write, "The Lord is my Shepherd; I shall not want" (Psalm 23:1). The Great Shepherd rescued him and brought him back into the fold.

Jesus Himself was a witness to adultery, the violence of hatred and the destruction of lives because of greed, lust, and jealousy. Nevertheless, He told it the way it was. The way of sin was eternal destruction. His way was the way of the more abundant life, eternally.

Several years ago I had the experience of driving on the Great Divide in the Rocky Mountains. I recalled, as we drove on this highway, that there the streams of water divided. Part of the water flows to the east and part to the west. The streams that flowed to the east were harnessed to grind the wheat into flour and aid in shipping on the Mississippi. On the other hand, until the Far West was settled, the streams that flowed in a westerly direction were not harnessed but raced on to the

Pacific, often causing flood and destruction. The waters came from the same origin. One was directed, the other uncontrolled.

The writer of Proverbs has said, "In all thy ways acknowledge him, and he shall direct thy paths" (Proverbs 3:6). A God-directed life brings peace of mind; the opposite, unhappiness. I, like many of you, chose the former and have never been disappointed.

HELPING OURSELVES

"The lord helps those who help themselves," admonished one of my favorite public-school teachers of long ago. It was his philosophy that no one should have done for him that which, by a little help, he could accomplish for himself. Even though this bit of wisdom may not be found in the Bible, the thought of it is there.

Little no good has come through our many welfare programs. While they are programs of sharing, they have been abused in many areas. There is no such thing as a free hand out. It costs someone along the way.

My mother and father agreed that my teacher was right, that the Lord helps those who help themselves. They saw to it that we applied this axiom in the home and on the farm. We were not to ask for help to do that which we could do for ourselves.

Have we not often taken the attitude of the little girl who lost her cat? It is said that she prayed, "Lord, You know that my cat is lost somewhere tonight. If You can't find her by morning, then I will start looking myself."

Jesus expected those whom He healed, if they were able, to cooperate. The Gospel-writer Matthew tells of the man with the withered hand. There was no question in the mind of Jesus about healing this man on the Sabbath day. He did ask that the man use his own strength and faith, saying unto him,

"... Stretch forth thine hand. And he stretched it forth; and it was restored whole, like as the other" (Matthew 12:13).

In His Sermon on the Mount, Jesus said, "Ask, and it shall be given you; seek, and ye shall find; knock, and it shall be opened unto you . . ." (Matthew 7:7). We grow by growing. It is a process that we can assist in or hinder. In any field of endeavor, we ourselves can do much in the process of growing.

God can use us only as we are willing to surrender what we have and place ourselves in His hands. He can then help us to make our lives an example for good.

Someone recently commented on my mother's influence on his life and said, "When your mother prayed, she seemed to bring heaven down to earth." I remarked, "It was because she spent so much time in the realm and atmosphere." The Lord helped her because she helped herself. He does this for each of us.

BALANCED RATIONS

For several years a windmill stood in our flower garden. I had worked for many hours to build it; it was about seven feet tall. I enjoyed watching it turn gaily in the wind.

One day after a storm, I noted that it had lost two of its blades. My windmill was out of balance without those blades. It ceased to run until I replaced them and it was once more in balance.

We hear much these days about *balanced rations*. We know how important they are to our health and to the pursuit of happiness.

When life gets out of balance, we are sure to have problems—physically, materially, and spiritually. We cannot afford to feed the physical at the expense of the mental, nor can we spend all our concerns on the material and starve the spiritual.

In speaking to His disciples and the multitude who had gathered on the hillside, Jesus told them that they should not worry about the material and physical so much that they neglected the spiritual. He concluded by advising, "... seek ye first the kingdom of God, and His righteousness; and all these things shall be added unto you" (Matthew 6:33).

Jesus knew the importance of our material needs, but He taught that we should seek first things first and then all the necessary tings of life would be supplied.

Many years ago I had the wedding of a fine young couple. Jack, upon returning from World War II, took over the farm of his parents. He and Margaret worked hard, and they reared a splendid family consisting of three sons and a daughter.

Little by little Jacks life broadened into many activities. I was called to the hospital one evening. He had been involved in a traffic accident, and for several days it was doubtful that he would recover.

As Jack grew stronger, he confided in me that he had prospered materially but had "drifted away from the God Who had helped him to prosper." He grasped my hand, and just before I prayed for him, he said, "I've had a lot of time to think as I have lain here. I've decided, by God's help, that I need to get things back in proper balance, as they were when Margaret and I were married. Pray that I may have the strength to do it."

Not only did God help Jack, but He can also help each of us to keep our life in proper balance as we seek first things first.

OCTOBER

Influencing Others

MOUNTAIN-TOP EXPERIENCES

We had just left Estes Park, Colorado, and were climbing the highway that leads to the Rocky Mountain National Park. The grandeur of the mountains above and the scenes of the valley below were breathtaking. I thought of the words of the vacation folder I had read a few weeks earlier: "A real vacation should inspire, not tire."

Mountain-top experiences come to us that we might better face the valleys of life with greater courage. Each of us has had inspiring experiences that we wished might go on—a good book, an inspirational musical program, a trip that we have made, or even a good sermon.

The Gospel according to Matthew tells us that Jesus took three of His disciples—Peter, James, and John—up into a high mountain. The experience of the miraculous transfiguration overwhelmed Peter. He was carried away with the scene and cried, "... Lord, it is good for us to be here: if thou wilt, let us make here three tabernacles; one for thee, and one for Moses, and one for Elias" (Matthew 17:4).

Peter wanted it to be a never-ending experience. He was saying, "Let us just stay here." Mountain-top experiences, however, are not only to enjoy, but to employ. They should not only inspire, but empower. God often gives us a glimpse of heaven that we might help to make earth better. We must return to the valley of service.

Recently a letter from a young mother told me of a heartwarming experience. "I am sure," she confided, "that experience was to prepare me for the loss of my infant son later that summer."

Bishop Matthew J. Shaw was a great man and an inspiring preacher. I heard him many times in my youthful days. He once related how, at the close of a service, a lady in the audience came by, shook his hand, and said, "Dr. Shaw, I'm going to treasure that sermon in my heart."

The great man looked down and responded with, "Is that all you are going to do with it?"

The mountain-top inspirations of life are shared with us so that we, in the Lord's name, might share them with others.

ENCOURAGE THE DISCOURAGED

For many years the motto of my life has been in the words of a poem, of which the author is unknown. The poem says,

> *If any little word of mine can make a life the brighter,*
> *If any little song of mine can make a heart the lighter,*
> *God help me speak that little word, and take my bit of singing*
> *And drop it in some lonely vale to set the echoes ringing.*

There is a second verse; without it, the first would not be complete.

If any little love of mine
May make a life the sweeter,
If any little care of mine
May make a friend's the fleeter,
If any little lift may ease
The burden of another,
God give me love and care
  and strength
To help my toiling brother.

It does not take a college degree nor a lot of money to be an encourager. It takes only a lot of love, concern, and understanding.

When Jesus was sending his disciples out, He gave them power for their mission. He said to them, "Heal the sick, cleanse the lepers, raise the dead, cast out devils: freely ye have received, freely give" (Matthew 10:8). To me, He was saying, "Go out and give hope to a discouraged world."

In the waiting room of a doctor's office, I once saw the following motto on the wall: "To cure sometimes—To relieve often—To comfort always." That motto was prepared and placed there many years ago by Dr. Robert McIlwain. It was his guiding principle, and he followed it faithfully in the encouragement of a host of people down through the years.

A man I recently met out in Indiana encouraged me when he said, "Your sermonettes have been like a guiding light on a dark road. They have encouraged me to go on."

Paul took the torch from his Lord and later wrote, "And now abideth faith, hope, charity, these three; but the greatest of these is charity" (I Corinthians 13:13).

The guiding motive of all encouragement should be love and charity. With that attitude in mind, we go out to share with others that which God hath shared with us in our Lord's name.

THE POWER OF EXAMPLE

"One action is worth a thousand words," so said the wise Benjamin Franklin. In response, we ask, "Who can measure the power of example?"

A famous English pastor, Charles Kingsley, once wrote, "There is nothing so infectious as example; you will do more good by doing good than in any other way."

A neighbor of mine during the early years of my ministry was a man of superb example. One day he laid his hand on my shoulder and said, "Don, always remember, you will preach a better sermon with your life than with your lips." The power of example cannot be measured.

Peter was invited to speack one day in the house of Cornelius the centurion. In the midst of his message, he spoke of the power of Jesus, ". . . who went about doing good. . ." (Acts 10:38). We know that the teaching ministry of Jesus made a tremendous and lasting impression in many ways, but his personal example—His life in action—had far greater effect.

To say "There goes a great orator" is not nearly as meaningful as to say "There goes a great Christian." The people of Boston who knew Phillips Brooks, a famous pastor of his day, said of him, "He lives what he preaches."

Jesus set us an example in public worship. "And he came to Nazareth, where he was brought up: and, as his custom was, he went into the synagogue on the sabbath day, and stood up for to read" (Luke 4:16).

At a good woman's funeral, the preacher declared, "Mary Holmes was a landmark on the highway of life in her church attendance."

Jesus set us an example in service too. He once proclaimed, ". . . the Son of man came not to be ministered unto, but to minister, and to give his life a ransom for many" (Matthew 20:28).

If we had the room, we could go on and remind ourselves of the power of Jesus in His example in prayer as well as His example in cross-bearing. Needless to say, He proved to us that the greatest power in one's life is the power of example. By His Presence in our lives, may we all be worthy examples.

AN ANTIDOTE FOR CONFUSION

Young Jimmie Martin was spending a few days with his grandparents. On Sunday morning Jimmie went to church with his grandfather. Grandmother was not feeling well and did not go.

At the dinner table, Grandma asked Jimmie how he liked the service. Jimmie replied, "The music was good. There were a lot of children and young people there." Then he concluded with, "I think there were ten who joined the church on confusion of faith." Although we know Jimmie meant *confession* of faith, there may have been some *confusion* of faith as well.

Recently former Senator Margaret Chase Smith was being interviewed. She said in part, "People today have lost their will. They are confused. They can't get the facts. They turn to the news media, then to Washington. They are totally different. In their confusion, they shrug their shoulders and say, 'Let the other fellow take care of it. It is too confusing for me.'"

Life can be either a battlefield or a peace conference. What is the formula? In the midst of our confusion, which way shall we turn?

The Psalm-writer had the answer. He prayed, "Teach me thy way, O Lord; I will walk in thy truth! unite my heart to fear thy name" (Psalm 86:11).

There is an old song that we have been singing for years. Every Billy Graham Crusade service closes with it. It was the true experience of Charolotte Elliott, who wrote the words. A part of one verse says, ... *Fightings within and fears without, O Lamb of God, I come.*

Many of us—in confusion, doubt, lack of confidence in the present and hope for the future—have found that turning it all over to God is the answer. As someone has said, "Let go—let

God." Might we add, "Confused? Don't despair. Turn to God in faith and prayer." He will always be our Guide in the presence of confusion.

A RECIPE FOR HAPPINESS

While I was on a speaking engagement down in Benton County, Indiana, the manager of a motel handed me a little card. On that card was what is called the "Happiness Recipe."

The formula reads, "Keep your heart free from hate, your mind from worry; Live simply, expect little, give much; Sing often, pray always, fill your life with love; Scatter sunshine, forget self, think of others. Do as you would be done by. These are the tried links in contentment's golden chain." He who welds together in his life this kind of chain is sure to experience true happiness.

The above is a tried and true recipe for happiness. Jesus, however, gave us the formula many centuries ago in His Sermon on the Mount, especially in the Beatitudes.

The "Happiness Recipe" is filled with positives. The Beatitudes likewise are positive. "Blessed are the merciful: for they shall obtain mercy" (Matthew 5:7). So taught the Master.

In our Lord's day, the way of the world was an eye for an eye and a tooth for a tooth. Hatred always led to more hatred. Every wrong always brought revenge. One day a young man came teaching a better way. Not a way of justice alone, but of mercy as well. People ridiculed this man. They crucified Him. But mercy and forgiveness—as Jesus taught and practiced— have long proven to bring as much peace of mind to the bestower as to the one who receives them.

I once read the story of a sheepowner who was plaqued by his neighbor's dogs, who were killing off his flock. Norman's procedure for curing the assault of the dogs called for fences, lawsuits, and shotgun blasts. But then he reached for a positive solution. He gave every neighbor's child a lamb as a pet. It was not long before those neighbors began to tie up their dogs, thus ending the problem.

Even a child knows the moral of these words: "Do good to them that hate you" (Matthew 5:44). Return good for evil. Show mercy instead of revenge. It works, not only with neighbors who harbor sheep-killing dogs but with people who have sharp, wounding tongues.

There are two words that stand out in the "Happiness Recipe." They are "Forget self." True happiness is not a selfish possession. It comes to us only when we forget ourselves and think of others. "Remember them that are in bonds, as bound with them; and them which suffer adversity..." (Hebrews 13:3). So advised the prophet of long ago. In practicing this kind of caring, we bring renewed hope to the hopeless and discover the happiness that is lasting.

GETTING ACQUAINTED

Getting acquainted is one of the enjoyable tasks we undertake when we move to a new neighborhood. "How well do you know your neighbors?" I asked a friend of mine who just six months earlier had moved to a new locality. He replied, "I have a speaking acquaintance with each of them." A speaking acquaintance is good, but to really get to know each other is better.

Uncle Orlo, my good neighbor, used to enjoy telling the story of the two maids who worked in adjacent homes. One of them reported an incident to her employer concerning the maid next door. She concluded by saying, "We have laughed together many times, but we never cried together until today." Aristotle said that people never really know each other until they have eaten a certain amount of salt together.

We hear much about the lack of communication these

days. With so many ways by which we may *communicate* with one another, one of the saddest failures of our world is that we have not learned to *understand* one another.

Little Mary was late for dinner. Her mother inquired concerning her tardiness, "Why are you late?" Mary replied, "Janie broke her doll's head, and I was helping her." Mother asked, "How did you help her?" The answer was, "I cried with her."

A "speaking acquaintance" is not enough. Only when we enter into the sorrows as well as the joys of others do we really learn to know one another.

The disciples were the Jesus for three years. They listened carefully as He spoke. They were amazed by the mircales He performed. They were impressed by His power of prayer. Through all of this, however, they did not learn to know Him as they might. Was it because they had not fully entered into His sorrows and concerns for the world? It was only when they began to realize the nature of His mission and the length to which He would go to complete it, that they began to know Him.

To become really acquainted with someone, we must have the experience of sitting where they sit, walking where they walk, and entering into their hopes and disappointments.

The Bible tells us Enoch. It says, "... And Enoch walked with God: and he was not; for God took Him" (Genesis 5:24). Enoch not only had a speaking acquaintance with the Lord, he took walks with Him. It was a common, everyday experience. They were friends.

It reminds me of the poet, Austris Wihtol, who wrote, "My God and I go in the fields together, we walk and talk as good friends should do." This closeness is the kind of friendship that each of us may experience. It is a fellowship that binds us together not only in the worship of our God but in love and understanding for one another.

THINGS THAT LAST

"In this world of change, naught which comes stays, naught which goes is lost," Shakespeare wrote long ago. In the last seventy years, many of us have seen more changes in our way of living than have people in any other age in history.

Some of us remember the first automobile, the first electric lights, the arrival of radio and television, the creation of the atomic bomb, and the first trip to the moon. These years have been eventful ones. And while many changes have contributed to the betterment of human welfare, not all change is beneficial progress.

It is refreshing in the midst of these changes to find that there are some things that are lasting. It is good to know that it is true that ". . . the light shineth in darkness; and the darkness comprehended it not" (John 1:5).

The unchanging Word supplies our needs in times of fear and sorrow. It gives expression to our greatest joys and leads us to peace of mind. It is the same yesterday, today, and forever.

The Ten Commandments, given unto Moses long ago, have never been improved upon. The Sermon on the Mount is as relevant today as when Jesus preached it centuries ago. Kingdoms and powers that vowed they would rule the world have come and gone. It seemed, at the time, that nothing could stand against them.

A baby was born in the village of Bethlehem. Evil powers tried to destroy Jesus from the time of His birth. These earthly powers had not counted on the powers of God, Who is from everlasting to everlasting.

Today where are the Caesars, the Napoleons, and other powers of tyranny? They are gone, their influence dwarfed, and we are still celebrating the birth and Resurrection of Jesus of Nazareth. We are the living witnesses of His teachings and the life He exemplified.

Other evil powers are in the present world, and others will come whose goal is to rule the world. But through all of these changes, we are fortified by the promise Jesus made to us when He said, "Heaven and earth shall pass away, but my words shall not pass away" (Matthew 24:35.)

JUNK, OR TREASURE?

"Your junk may be someone else's treasure," the auctioneer told us. We were moving, and we were having to give up many of our belongings collected through the years. The man with the auction company was loading onto the truck the possessions we hoped to sell.

Surveying the items, I said, "Some of this is nothing more than junk." It was then that the auctioneer made his comment, adding, "It all depends on the possibilities a prospective buyer sees in your so-called junk."

I have often wondered where most of us would be today if someone else had not minimized our mistakes and weaknesses and emphasized our possibilities. No doubt God saw in Moses a poor, stammering, fearful young man. But He also saw in him the ability to be a great leader.

Some of the so-called religious and educated men of Jesus's day thought that He was wasting His time on the outcasts of the land. They saw these poor folk as they were, not as what they could become.

Many years ago in a little village in Wales, a widowed mother who was very poor awoke one morning to find her baby boy seriously ill. The nearest doctor was ten miles away. Leaving the infant in the care of a neighbor, she set out on foot to get the doctor.

Even though the physician knew that he would not receive his fee, he also knew that here was a human being in need. Like many other compassionate doctors of that day and today, he answered the call for help.

The baby lived. Years later he became Prime Minister of Great Britain. His name was David Lloyd George. It is not so much from whence we have come or what we have been but what we—through the concern of others and with the grace of God—can be that counts.

Each one of the disciples of Jesus was, by himself, a failure. But when the high priests and rulers interrogated Peter and John, "... [they] perceived that they were unlearned and ignorant men, they marvelled; and they took knowledge of them, that they had been with Jesus" (Acts 4:13).

Yes, our junk may be someone else's treasure. Jesus forgives us the "junk" of our errors and emphasizes the "treasures" of our potential. We should never underestimate the power of God and the loving concern of others in the future of a human life.

GOD GIVES THE INCREASE

I found myself bragging somewhat as I showed our visitors our peaches, grapes, raspberries, and tomatoes. The plants had never looked better. Fruit hung heavy on the branches and vines. I had given them tender, loving care. I had pruned them, sprayed, fertilized, and watered them. We began early to enjoy the results of our labor.

As I pondered over the success of our small but fruitful venture, a voice seemed to say, "Don, you have planted and you have cared for your garden, but God has given the increase."

We hear so often when a disaster such as a flood, tornado, or snowstorm strikes, "The are acts of God." Be that as it may, I have frequently wondered if we fail to see that the bountiful harvests are also acts of God.

Paul gave us words of wisdom when he said to the Christians at Corinth, "I have planted, Apollos watered; but God gave the increase" (I Corinthians 3:6).

One of Aesop's fables tells of a frog and two geese. Each of the geese held one end of a stick in its mouth, and they agreed to let the frog grasp the stick in its middle so that he might fly with them. As they flew over a farmyard, the farmer called out, "Whose idea was that?" The frog shouted, "It was my idea." And as he opened his mouth to brag of his wisdom, he lost his grasp on the stick and fell to the ground.

I often think of how little we could really accomplish by ourselves alone. We are like links in the great chain of life's events. Others before us, or beside us, plant. We come along and help in the continuing process of life's plan, but God giveth the increase.

I look back over these many years. If I have had a small part in encouraging someone along the way, it has not been through my own ability. Rather, it has been that God has spoken through me. He has given the increase. I would have failed long ago without Him.

Jesus, in the last earthly hours with His disciples there in the Upper Room, counseled them to remember, "I am the vine, ye are the branches: He that abideth in me, and I in him, the same bringeth forth much fruit: for without me ye can do nothing" (John 15:5).

Whether we be growing the fruits of the field or the fruits of our lives, it is God working through each of us Who giveth the increase. Without Him, all would be a disaster. With him, the fruits of life will prosper.

NOVEMBER

Counting Our Blessings

IN GRATITUDE FOR OUR HERITAGE

Recently ninety-eight members of the Jennings family gathered for their annual family reunion. It was many years ago that Oscar M. and Minnie Jennings took up residence in Wayne County, Indiana, near the little town of Whitewater. There they made a life and a living for a family that grew in numbers through the years.

It took a lot of sharing and caring over the course of that time. This can well be illustrated by how my brother Glen and I, as ten- and twelve-year-old brothers, learned to use the crosscut saw. Each of us was blaming the other for the saw's not running smoothly. Our father came over to where we were working. He laid his hands on us and said, "Boys, you have to pull and push *together*." Needless to say, we learned the secret. In so doing, we—along with other members of the family—were able to cut twenty cords of wood that August.

Many times since then I have felt the continuing influence in my life of those wise and concerned parents, and I have been forever grateful for that heritage.

As American citizens, we have paused year after year to celebrate Thanksgiving Day. I have observed that it can best be celebrated as a family day. God has blessed the home and the family. We read, "God setteth the solitary in families..." (Psalm 68:6), and "... [he] maketh him families like a flock" (Psalm 107:41).

We first learn the meaning of gratitude as children in the home and around the table. Gratitude is, or should be, a heritage passed on from generation to generation by loving parents and relatives.

Thanksgiving is a national holiday. "Blessed is the nation whose God is the Lord..." (Psalm 33:12). Those words are as true today as when they were written by the Psalm-writer long ago.

Our beloved nation was founded upon a faith in and a dependance on the providence of God. Even though we may not have been worthy at times of God's blessings, He has continued to nourish and sustain us. We are rich in natural resources. We have many freedoms not afforded by some nations of the world. Among our freedoms is the priceless right to worship by the dictates of our own conscience.

We come once again to the Thanksgiving season. As we do so, we will do well if in addition to our daily acknowledgement of gratitude, we count our blessings and give special thankfulness to God for our rich heritage.

THINK, THEN THANK

It was Thanksgiving Eve. A light snow was falling and darkness was gathering as we slowly made our way through the village. At the end of the street, set deep amongst the evergreens, was a small, white church. In front of the church was a well-lit bulletin board on which I read the words: "If you think, you will thank."

A man of many winters once said to me, "The reason we are often thankless is that we are often thoughtless." I have observed that the machinery of life runs much more smoothly if it is generously lubricated with the oil of gratitude.

Thanksgiving is one of our most sacred holidays. It is a day when we confess our limitations without God and realize our possibilities with His help. It is a day when we pause to express our gratitude to God for His bountiful blessings to us. Many of us have discovered that true Thanksgiving cannot be saved up for just one day.

It would seem to me today that our Puritan forefathers had very little for which to be thankful on that first Thanksgiving. But they did give thanks, not only for their blessings but for the dangers from which they had escaped.

One of the most familiar Psalms for giving thanks is Psalm 103. The second verse says, "Bless the Lord, O my soul, and forget not all his benefits."

"If we think, we will thank," so proclaimed the bulletin board on that snowy night. Remembering to be thankful for small blessings increases their value. In fact, as we express our gratitude, we come to realize that there are no small blessings. Being thankful makes our blessings doubly blessed.

This Thanksgiving as we gather around our tables spread with the bounties of life, we can do no less than to thank God for His goodness and share with those who are less fortunate than we. As we do this our own blessings will mean much more to us, and we will realize what Jesus meant when He said, "... Inasmuch as ye have done it unto one of the least of these my brethren, ye have done it unto me" (Matthew 25:40).

PRAYER, THE LIFELINE

Many years ago, during a time of mental and spiritual depression, I read the words, "Keep a firm grip on prayer and God will see you through." It was at about this same time that Romans 8:28 was gradually becoming my favorite Bible verse. It reads, "And we know that all things work together for good to them that love God, to them who are called according to his purpose."

During those days I was forced to turn to a higher power than myself. It was then that I learned to pray, "Lord, without Thee, I will utterly fail; with Thee, I cannot fail." I have never ceased to pray that prayer. It has been my vital lifeline to God.

I realized that spending more time in prayer, and then putting my faith to work, gave me strength to quiet my fears and encourage my endeavors. Someone has said that prayer never becomes a vital part of life until we reserve a place for it in our daily living.

Do the pressures of life, at times, seem to almost overwhelm you, as they nearly did me many years ago? Keep a firm grip on prayer, and God will see you through.

Paul, when sharing his spiritual wisdom with the early Christians, wrote, "Pray without ceasing" (I Thessalonians 5:17). Whatever the burden, whatever the pressures of life may be, whatever the decisions that need to be made—keep in a spirit of prayer. Keep the lifeline open to God.

Even Jesus felt the need for prayer and knew its importance. When the pressures were more than He could bear alone, when His life was being threatened by His enemies, He sought solitude Luke says that ". . . it came to pass in those days, that he went out into a mountain to pray, and continued all night in prayer to God" (Luke 6:12).

We all need a mountain, a quiet place away from the noise of the day, a place where we can lay our burdens and our hopes at the feet of the One Who understands—He Who can give us renewed faith and courage for the days ahead.

Prayer is not giving up but giving over to God as we relinquish our will to His will. It is truly the Lifeline for all who will, in faith, reach for it.

TIME FOR PRAISE

*This is my Father's world.
The birds their carols raise
The morning light,
The lily white,
Declare their Maker's praise.*

So writes Maltbie Babcock, an American poet, in the hymn we all enjoy singing.

Praise is not an unnatural response for blessings received, but a spontaneous show of gratitude. On the other hand, critics are necessary sentinels along the highways of our lives. They challenge us to do our best. Criticism is often like bitter medicine, unpleasant to take but necessary for the improvement of our health.

A word of praise to a child who is trying to do his best encourages him to do even better. Henry Ward Beecher, famous American pastor and author, said, "There is not a person in our employ who does not desire recognition and praise."

The praise of others may be of use in teaching us not what we are but what we might be. A wise man of long ago worte, "Let another man praise thee, and not thine own mouth; a stranger, and not thine own lips" (Proverbs 27:2).

Most of us have accomplished little within our own power, and that which we did accomplish was due to God, working through us. One translation of the story of Gideon's defeat of the Midianites says that the "Spirit of the Lord clothed Himself with Gideon." The real praise was to God, Who used Gideon.

When I was growing up, we had a pastor who influenced my future more than any other preacher I know. The Rev. L. F. Ulmer, his faithful wife, and his talented daughter Ruth could make music as I imagine the music of heaven must sound. Whenever anyone would compliment this inspiring man on his family's music or on his preaching, he would always say, "Well, praise the Lord."

I used to think that when he preached, he was shouting or being emotional. Later I discovered that he *meant* it when he said, "Give the praise to the Lord. We are just His instruments, through which He sings, plays, and speaks."

We used to sing a song, a part of which one verse said,

Do then the best you can,
Not for reward,
Not for the praise of man,
But for the Lord.

When we give our best by God's help, we need not be concerned about praise from man. We have the approval of God.

HUMBLE GRATITUDE

In 1795, President Washington asked the nation to observe a day of Thanksgiving. He urged the people to gather in their churches, to humbly and fervently pray to God that He might prolong the blessings bestowed upon this nation, and to ask God to imprint in their hearts a deep and solemn sense of their obligation to Him for those blessings. Washington closed his plea with these words: "And finally, impart all the blessings we possess, or ask for ourselves, to the whole family of mankind."

Appreciation means expressing our gratitude to Him Who has provided for us so bountifully. But it goes beyond that, for our blessings mean so much more when we share them with others.

That first Thanksgiving at Plymouth was a time of showing humble appreciation to God. It was an occasion in which our Pilgrim fathers shared what little they had with their friendly Indian neighbors. They did not join together to bewail their grief but to show their gratitude. They did not complain of the past; they prayed for God's blessing on their future.

Our nation has come far since the first Thanksgiving, and God has blessed the years in many ways. Somewhere along the line, however, we have lost sight or some of the principles most needed for our nation's good. We have become rich in material things, in technology, and in scientific achievement. We have become a powerful nation, rich with implements for waging war but weak in wisdom with which to make and keep the peace. There are those within our borders who have not realized that there can be no individual freedom without an orderly society.

It is not too late to return to those principles that once made our country an influence for good in the world. We have the skills and know-how to do much. Many great and noble advances are being made. But one of our greatest needs is for courageous humility—for a confession that even with all we possess and all we are endeavoring to do, we fail miserably if we do not acknowledge our dependence upon God.

The promise of God to King Solomon of Old Testament days is as valid today as it was centuries ago. In response to Solomon's prayer, God answered, "If my people, which are called by my name, shall humble themselves, and pray, and seek my face, and turn from their wicked ways; then will I hear from heaven, and will forgive their sin, and will heal their land" (II Chronicles 7:14).

As we pause to show our gratitude for the many blessings God has bestowed upon us, we will do well to humbly ask His forgiveness. Let us pray for wisdom and courage, that we may each help to make our nation yet become the land God would have it to be.

RETURNING THANKS

Although Thanksgiving Day is another of our national holidays, each of us knows that it is really more than that. True thanksgiving is an attitude of the heart and cannot be saved up for one day only.

We are often so busy enjoying our blessings that we forget to show our gratitude. I am reminded of the husband who was enjoying a special dish his wife had prepared. As he ate heartily, his wife asked, "George, how do you like the special dish I prepared?" Without looking up, George replied, "I'm eating, aren't I?"

The Psalm-writer gave us the following familiar words long ago: "Bless the Lord, O my soul, and forget not all his benefits" (Psalm 103:2). God has blessed we Americans as no nation of people has ever before been blessed. We will do well to "forget not all his benefits."

I once saw a cartoon of a man sitting at a table that was spread with food. With his napkin tucked under his chin, he surveys the bounty before him, then exclaims, "What, no flowers?"

The Gospel according to Luke tells of Jesus meeting ten lepers on His way to Jerusalem. In response to their cry for mercy, He said to them, "Go show yourselves unto to the priests. And it came to pass, that, as they went, they were cleansed" (Luke 17:14). One of the ten, when he saw that he was healed, returned to give thanks. Jesus asked him, "... were there not ten cleansed? but where are the nine?" (Luke 17:17).

The best part of giving thanks is what it does for us. "... thy faith hath made thee whole," said Jesus (Luke 19:19). The leper, in reward for his spirit of thanksgiving, was not only cleansed of his leprosy, but his life was made whole. This is what happens to us when we sincerely return thanks.

In these days when so many people seem to forget God and His many blessings, some even making light of the Divine Creator, it is all the more urgent that we observe a truly meaningful Thanksgiving Day. Feasting and other social activities, as much as we may enjoy them, can never be a substitute for giving thanks to God for our Divine heritage.

EVALUATING OUR WANTS

A boy of twelve who was an admirer of Abraham Lincoln often noted the long legs of his hero and lamented on how short he himself was for a lad of his age. One day he asked Lincoln, "Mr. Lincoln, for a boy of my age, how long should my legs be?"

Mr. Lincoln smiled and answered, "Son, only long enough to reach the ground."

There is a difference between our necessities and our desires. Our economy in America is based on a policy of plenty, not of sustenance.

When the Psalm-writer said, "The Lord is my shepherd; I shall not want" (Psalm 23:1), he was not speaking of human desires alone but of spiritual necessities as well.

As a young lad at home on the farm many years ago, I did not have everything that I wanted, but everything that I needed. I suppose that in the light of today's material values, we lived in poverty. I did not find this out, however, until I was forty years of age. Then I thanked God that I had had parents who believed and taught that "... Man shall not live by bread alone" (Matthew 4:4).

We can have freedom from want only as we discover the difference between our wants and our necessities; and if as a nation we are to continue to have freedom from want, we must be vigilant. Some of us remember the slogans of World War II that called our attention to the need for vigilance. One such slogan was, "Willful waste brings woeful want." Another, "Is this trip necessary?"

Many times Jesus taught the importance of being watchful. On that sad, yet eventful night in Gethsemane, when Jesus returned from praying, He found three of His most trusted disciples asleep. Turning to Peter, He said, "... What, could ye not watch with me one hour? Watch and pray, that ye enter not into temptation: the spirit indeed is willing, but the flesh is weak" (Matthew 26:40-41).

Last, but far from least, to assure freedom from want, we must discover the Source Who fulfills our needs. Paul assured the early Christians, "... my God shall supply all your needs according to his riches in glory by Christ Jesus" (Philippians 4:19).

In the parable of the Prodigal Son, it seemed that the son had everything but freedom to do as he pleased. In his willfulness, he failed to evaluate his needs. He did not realize how well off he really was, and he failed to practice vigilance. He squandered and dissipated all that had been given him. But in his time of awakening, he did not forget to whom to turn to find his true freedom. The best decision he ever made was to return to his father's house.

Our Heavenly Father has the answer to all our needs.

EXPRESSING OUR GRATITUDE

"Expressing our gratitude increases the value of our blessings," my good friend and neighbor, Uncle Orlo, philosophized as we surveyed our gardens. We were lamenting the failure of the early vegetables but thankful for the good pumpkins. I responded with, "Uncle Orlo, if we can't be thankful for what we have, we can at least be thankful for what we have escaped."

There is an old Aesop fable that tells of a dog carrying a bone in his mouth as he crosses a footbridge over a small stream. As the dog looks down, he sees his image in the water. Thinking it to be another dog with a bone in his mouth, he wants that bone also. The dog on the bridge barks at his image and loses the bone he had.

Sometimes gratitude is felt most profoundly when we measure our blessings and compare them with those who are less fortunate than we.

I once heard of a man and his wife who had lately come to America. He obtained a position as night watchman at a public school near their home. It did not pay much, but it was a job.

He lost the job, however, when it was learned that he could not read. Not to be defeated, this man and his wife opened a small hamburger stand. His business grew, as did his bank account. One day his banker friend called him in and said, Frank, you are doing real well, but think of where you might be if you could read." Frank responded with, "If I could read, I'd still be a night watchman at the neighborhood school." We can be thankful for failure in one endeavor of life if it leads us to do better in another.

"Make the best of the worst," advised a woman who was blind but who had an undefeatable outlook on life. This was also the philosophy of Paul. In prison and with death threatening him, he wrote to his friends in the church at Philippi, "... I have learned, in whatsoever state I am, therewith to be content" (Philippians 4:11).

Our country was founded upon a realistic acceptance of our oftentimes precarious situation, being thankful for the bitter along with the sweet, and sharing our blessings with others.

As we come to another Thanksgiving season, might it not be well that we, like the Psalm-writer, determine to express our gratitude in deed as well as word as we say, "Bless the Lord, O my soul, and forget not all his benefits . . ." (Psalm 103:2). My friend Uncle Orlo was right: "Expressing our gratitude increases the value of our blessings."

RAINBOWS

"Daddy, what's a rainbow?" questioned little six-year-old Millis.

Her father, a science teacher in the local high school, replied, "Millie, a rainbow is an arc of prismatic colors seen at those times when the sun shines while it is raining. It is caused by the reflection and refraction of the rays of the sunlight in the drops of rain."

Six-year-old Millis was quiet for a few moments. Then she

responded with, "Oh, so that's it. Well, our teacher said that God placed the rainbow in the clouds following the great flood. It was His promise that the world would never be drowned by a flood again."

Both the father, with his scientific explanation, and little Millis, explaining her teacher's definition, were right.

I do not recall when I first saw a rainbow, but I remember seeing many of them down through the years. It is good to remember that since the beginning of time, rainbows have followed the storms. They are another one of God's miracles of beauty and hope.

The book of Genesis tells us that God made a covenant with Noah and his sons following the flood and sealed it by setting His rainbow in the cloud: There He told Noah, "And it shall come to pass, when I bring a cloud over the earth, that the bow shall be seen in the cloud..." (Genesis 9:14). Neither the rainbow nor God's covenent have faded or failed down through the years.

Following a recent speaking engagement, I was approached by a young woman who shook my hand. With tearms in her eyes but a radiant smile on her face, she witnessed to her faith. She told me of the sad loss of one of her two daughters. "But," she continued, "I have found that in back of every cloud, the sun is shining and the rainbow waits our reaching out for it." As she talked, I saw the reflection of the rainbow of hope in her countenance and her courageous faith in God, Who had stood beside her.

How often the storms of life seem to threaten our very existence! We are about ready to give up. Then the rainbow of hope, that reflection of God's love, bids us look up, and we realize that His covenant is true, "... for he hath said, I will never leave thee, nor forsake thee" (Hebrews 13:5).

This has been the promise of God to men and women of faith from the beginning. It is as the eternal rainbow that never fails to shine through life's clouds.

LONELINESS, OR SOLITUDE?

"Loneliness is the sad weeping of the heart, solitude the searching of the mind." I used those words in a radio broadcast many years ago. Following the broadcast, a listener sent me the following: "A person who spends his time building walls instead of bridges has no right to complain if he is lonely."

Who has not, at times and often through no fault of his own, felt the aching pangs of loneliness? One does not need to be alone to experience loneliness. Some of us have known loneliness in its most devastating degree when we were in a crowd where no one seemed to share our feelings. Loneliness is the condition of our hearts and minds more than the place wherein we find ourselves.

Recently a mother whose responsibilities are many asked, "Do you think that Jesus was ever lonely?" I replied, "Yes, I think that He must have been." Then we talked of how we would have felt had we carefully chosen twelve companions, only to have one of them betray us, another deny us, and three of them go to sleep while we were fighting our greatest battle, alone, in prayer.

"What do you do when you are loney?" I asked this mother. Her answer was, "I find a place of solitude. There in the quietness, I search out my heart and receive strength from Jesus, Who also felt the need of solitude at times. Then I leave the solitude to go help someone—a member of my family or a neighbor—and my loneliness melts away."

Solitude is often an experience over which we have no control. On the other hand, it is also an experience for which we feel a need. In either case, in solitude the searching mind gains strength and learns to lean upon itself, by the help of God. In solitude we take time to examine ourselves and to learn God's will for the problems or opportunities that lie ahead of us. Most of the world's progress has come out of solitude.

In Old Testament days there was an occasion described by

the following words, which have great meaning for us today, "And Jacob was left alone..." (Genesis 32:24). Out of that loneliness and solitude came repentance, forgiveness, and victory for Jacob and those who would follow after him.

Aloneness is an important part of the lives of poets, scientists, inventors, our spiritual leaders, and the multitude of men and women like you and me. Let us accept it, and be thankful.

BELIEFS FOR SALE

The farm auction was about to begin. The farmer announced, "Everything you see here goes to the highest bidder." A nearby onlooker turned to me and said, "There seem to be plenty of folk these days who are ready to sell even their beliefs to the highest bidder."

Everyone may be tempted, at some time in his life, to sell his beliefs. There are those who are willing to sell anything they have to the highest bidder.

The wise author of Proverbs once wrote, "Buy the truth, and sell it not..." (Proverbs 23:23). But there are those who are tempted to sell the truth, to their later sorrow and the disappointment of others.

What is a belief? Some say it is our creed, or the sum of our convictions. Someone has observed that it is not so much what one believes, but how one lives that counts. I am convinced, however, that to a large extent what one believes determines how one lives.

The woman whom Matthew tells of had been ill for many years. She held fast to her belief. One day when Jesus was in her town, she said to herself, "... If I may but touch his garment, I shall be whole" (Matthew 9:21). She did and she was.

Why would one be tempted to sell his or her beliefs? Esau sold his belief in the value of his birthright for a mess of pottage. Judas sold his belief in Jesus as the Messiah for thirty pieces of silver.

Jesus said to His disciples one day, "For what is a man profited, if he shall gain the whole world, and lose his own soul..." (Matthew 16:26). One sells his beliefs only when he fails to recognize their value. There is no profit in bartering our future security to satisfy our present desires. Beliefs should not be for sale; they are for our security and peace of mind. They are our eternal values.

A mother had worked hard and sacrificed much for her family. Her husband had died early and left her with three children to rear and educate. Her faith did not waver through all the years. The oldest son, whom she was helping to attend the university, came home to the farm for his vacation. One evening he informed his mother that he had learned that man was becoming self-sufficient and that faith in God was no longer necessary.

"Son," responded the mother, "the doctor tells me I am dying. If I accept your belief, what have you to offer me now?"

As the son left the house, not knowing what to say, he heard his mother singing, "All the way my Saviour leads me, What have I to ask besides..."

The person who told me this story concluded it with, "That woman was my mother. My faith is what it is today because my mother held to her belief." Yes, our belief in God, through Christ, is not for sale, for it is the finest legacy we possess to hand on to those who follow us.

DECEMBER

Taking the Road to Bethlehem

THE CHRISTMAS PAUSE

It was Christmas Eve, 1914. World War I was at its height. Young men far from home huddled in their trenches. Remembering the day, someone started to hum "Silent Night, Holy Night." Soon others in the regiment were singing the familiar hymn. When the last refrain had died away, voices from the German trenches across the way took up the singing of "Stille Nacht."

On into the night Christmas carols rang from trench to trench, in strange tongues but with the same spirit and hope. After the "zero" hour, the fighting was resumed, but for a time at least, the war had been forgotten while all united in the music of Christmas.

I heard this story in my youth from a veteran who was fortunate enough to return from the war. He concluded by saying, "The music on that Christmas Eve had softened their hatred, and for that brief time, they were just two groups of homesick boys on Christmas Eve."

How many times events like unto this have been related. One wonders why, if the world can pause for a while in peace on Christmas Eve, that peace cannot continue. If man would only let the love that came to earth on the first Christmas Day overcome the hatred that seems to rule his heart, there could be a lasting peace.

The message of the angel at that blessed event still inspires and gives hope to a darkened world with "Glory to God in the highest, and on earth peace, good will toward men."

Christmas comes to us at a time when often the powers of hatred and greed are gambling for the souls and lives of men. This was true at the time of the first Christmas. There were no freedoms in the dark night when Jesus came to set men free. Let us not forget that the angelic song of peace and good will came during a brief lull in centuries of fighting.

Could it be that the world may someday catch on to the real truth of that first Christmas Day? Only when man allows the Christ Child be born anew within him will the Christmas pause lengthen into a true world brotherhood.

Even as I write this, I seem to hear those who say that all of this is good but it will never work. This was what they said about Jesus and his ideals. Down through the centuries, however, many have discovered that it does work.

I am sure that there are some of you, like me, who will pause under the spell of another Christmas Day. Even though many families will be separated because of war, sickness, and mistakes, let us all turn to the great Prince of Peace and pray that the world, in our time, may catch the true meaning of His coming.

MAKE ROOM FOR CHRISTMAS

A merchant friend of mine was rearranging the display in the front window of his store. I stopped to watch him. He noticed my interest and motioned for me to come inside. As I entered, he exclaimed, "We have to make room for Christmas!"

Even though he was speaking commercially, there was more truth in his words than he realized. Christmas is indeed an occasion for which we have to make room.

I never hear the Christmas story read but what I listen as though an old and favorite hymn were being sung again. One Christmas Eve I observed a young mother as she read the Christmas story to her three young children. Their eyes and ears were alert. They listened as though they had never heard the story before. As I listened I made some observations, which I pass along to you.

As Christmas approaches, we must make room for joy. Christmas is, or should be, a joyful time. The angel said, "Fear not: for, behold, I bring you good tidings of great joy, which shall be to all people" (Luke 2:10).

Did you ever stand by, watch, and listen as people do their Christmas shopping? One day I looked on as an exasperated mother lamented, "I'm glad Christmas comes but once a year. Jane, do you have an aspirin?"

I observed that not all of the shoppers were like this woman, though. As a helpful clerk wrapped a gift for a boy in his early teens, she said, "This is a pretty nice gift for your mother." The boy, with a beaming smile, replied, "I have a pretty nice mother." Joy comes to us at Christmas as we bring it to others. This joy is not found in the price tag on the gift but by the love in our hearts.

Someone has said that Christmas is not Christmas unless we make room for little children. Most of us have watched the hope and expectation in a child's face on Christmas Eve. If you have not seen that hope and felt the tug of a child's hand on Christmas morning, you have missed one of the glowing wonders of life.

We can never forget that a little child was the center of the first eventful Christmas. The Christmas story tells us that the shepherds "... found Mary, and Joseph, and the babe lying in a manger" (Luke 2:16).

Soon it will again be Christmas in millions of homes. Families and kinsmen will gather around the table. They will eat a little more than is good for them, and the warmth of human kindness will shine forth. Will it end there?

If we make adequate preparation for Christmas, we will hear His voice again as He tells us, "Inasmuch as ye have done it unto one of the least of these my brethren, ye have done it unto me" (Matthew 25:40).

We will then see the world and its needs through His eyes. In so doing, we will have truly more room for Christmas.

JOY TO THE WORLD

"Joy to the world! The Lord is come"; wrote Isaac Watts, English hymn-writer. With those words he was inspired to compose one of our most familiar Christmas carols, "Joy to the World." Most of us learned it in childhood, and it is traditional that we sing it throughout each Christmas season. It is not only traditional, it speaks of the answer to the hope of the ages.

It was during World War II that an English father was walking the darkened streets of London with a friend. This father had already lost one son in the war. His second son was somewhere in battle on the mainland of Europe. As these two fathers, each on rescue duty in darkened London, made their way through the bomb-wrecked streets, the first father said, "The lights have gone out in our world, and I wonder if they will ever come on again."

This was the question in the minds of many people in the "blackout" days of that terrible war. It was also the question asked by many generations long before the glorious night of which Isaac Watts wrote.

Where there are those who live in despair, there are also those who have not lost hope.

The prophet by the name of Isaiah was certain that "in the fullness of time" God would come to redeem His people from slavery, sorrow, sin, and death. Isaiah wrote of that day when he said, "The people that walked in darkness have seen a great light: they that dwell in the land of the shadow of death, upon them hath the light shined" (Isaiah 9:2).

Isaiah predicted also that a child would be born who would be called "... wonderful, Counsellor, The mighty God, The everlasting Father, The Prince of Peace" (Isaiah 9:6).

Each year as Christmas draws near, we read again of the coming of the Prince of Peace. The lights of hope seem to burn a little brighter, and there is a quickening of the spirit of kindness and love.

We seem to be led once more to the little town of Bethlehem. We hear again the angel's song, "On earth peace, good will toward men." Violence and indifference are overshadowed by love, forgiveness, and compassion. We find ourselves drawn a little closer to one another as well make room for the Prince of Peace. The darkened streets of our hearts are brightened with the renewed spirit of faith, hope, and love. Joy to the world. The Lord is come!

THE HOPE OF BETHLEHEM

"The hopes and fears of all the years are met in thee tonight," Phillips Brooks wrote as he looked out over Bethlehem on a Christmas Eve many years ago.

As we come to another Christmas season, our hopes turn to Bethlehem. Bethlehem is just another town, except for the event that came to pass there two thousand years ago—the birth of Christ, the Saviour. There is nothing special about an old wooden cross either, except that it was on that cross that Jesus died that we might live. Joseph's tomb was like many others of that day, except that from that tomb came the risen Christ to give renewed hope to all who sorrow.

The hope that was born in Bethlehem was the hope of true joy. The Heavenly angels electrified the air above the hillsides outside Bethlehem by saying, "... behold, I bring you good tidings of great joy ..." (Luke 2:10). The event at Bethlehem was to bring lasting joy to all who would accept it.

Second, the hope that was born that night at Bethlehem was the hope of eternal peace. What a mighty chorus was that "multitude of heavenly host" as they sang "Glory to God in the highest, and on earth peace, good will toward men" (Luke 2:14).

According to the angels, good will toward others helps to bring peace. There is no time of the year when good will is more prevalant than at Christmastime. Heart strings as well as purse strings are loosened at Christmas. But the hope born at Bethlehem was for peace amongst our fellow man from that time forward.

That leads us to say that the hope of Bethlehem was the hope for eternity. Hope is the window by which we see through a glass darkly into the eternal plans of God. Before Jesus, one generation after another had looked forward with hope but lived in the shadows of fear. Then He came! The people who had walked in darkness now had a great light.

Yes, Phillips Brooks was right: "The hopes and fears of all the years are met in Thee tonight."

Because of that which came to pass at Bethlehem, Christmas now means Joy, Peace, and Eternal Hope. With renewed faith, then, we can sing, "O come, let us adore Him, Christ the Lord."

HOW?

As a lad growing up on the farm, I was responsible for looking after the dairy cattle and the milking. We had a cow we called

Inkie. We gave her this name because she was a beautiful black. In my young mind, it was always a mystery how this black cow could eat green grass and produce white milk that made yellow butter. This mystery, however, did not keep me from enjoying her finished product.

There are many mysteries in the physical, material, and spiritual worlds that I cannot fully understand. I accept what I can by reason and the rest by faith.

In the Gospel according to John, the author tells us that a man by the name of Nicodemus, a ruler of the Jews, came to Jesus by night. This man, who had seen many of the miracles performed by our Master, could not understand His power.

Jesus talked to Nicodemus about "being born again," and Nicodemus questioned, "How can these things be?" (John 3:9). He was an honest man, and the question, "How?" concerned him.

Man has since learned many of the answers to the question, "How?" But there are other mysteries we must accept by faith. A greater power holds within His hands the answers to these mysteries. That power is God, Creator of all that is good.

Many of us enjoy singing,

O Lord my God,
When I in awesome wonder
Consider all the worlds Thy hands have made,
I see the stars,
I hear the rolling thunder,
Thy power throughout the universe displayed.

The above words by Stuart K. Hine tell us that the answers are with God and through God.

What one of us has not often noticed a change for the better in the lives, actions, and personalities of some of those around us? Someone, seeing the mysterious changes, asks the question, "How can these things be?" We know the answer;

Paul has written, "Therefore if any man be in Christ, he is a new creature: old things are passed away; behold, all things are become new" (II Corinthians 5:17). The changed man is never the same again. He has new appetites, new goals, a new partnership. His entire life is changed.

When some tragedy crosses our pathway, it is natural for us to ask, "Why?" and, "How can this work together for our good?"

Might not the answer be found in this bit of verse that came to me recently?

It is not for us to question
How? Dear Lord.
Why the pain? the chastening rod?
It is only as we do the things we must
That we learn the answer from simple trust.
God holds within His hands the key.

TODAY

Nostalgia is the "in" word. Many articles, books, television series, and other avenues of communication about the "good old days" seem to be popular these days. "Nostalgia," says Noah Webster, "is a wistful ... or sentimental ... yearning for the past or irrecoverable condition." The nostalgic mind has as its theme, "Those were the days."

Some of us who lived in those good old days agree that those days are often more interesting to talk about or write about than to live over again, even if we could. True, life was slower then, but it was not always easier, for much of the work of the good old days was back-breaking.

As I say in my book *A Time to Remember*, "Yesterday is only a memory away, and in memory is about the only way that we can go back and live those days over again."

It does us little good to worry about the mistakes of

yesterday any more than it does to be overly concerned about what tomorrow will bring. Yesterday has passed forever beyond our control. We may profit by its mistakes, which will help us do better tomorrow.

Tomorrow is also beyond our immediate control. Tomorrow is the today that we worried about yesterday.

Dear Uncle Orlo, my good neighbor of yesteryear, once said, "It is not the day or the age but the attitude or the spirit that help us to see that we can live only one day at a time." Yes, the Psalmist was right when he said, "This is the day which the Lord hath made; we will rejoice and be glad in it" (Psalm 118:24).

Uncle Orlo was right too. We can live only one day at a time. We cannot possibly bear the remorse of yesterday's mistakes and the worries about tomorrow and still meet, victoriously, the opportunities of today. If we "rejoice" in this day and do, by God's help, what our hands find to do, we will be storing up hopes for tomorrow and its needs.

The poet Ernest R. Wilberforce once wrote:

Lord, for tomorrow and its needs, I do not pray.
Keep me, my God, from stain of sin just for day.

As we know, Jesus taught us not to be overly concerned about tomorrow. He said, ". . . for the morrow shall take thought for the things of itself. Sufficient unto the day is the evil thereof" (Matthew 6:34).

This is the day the Lord has made for us. We will be grateful for this day, and we pray that with the setting of the sun, we may turn the key in the lock and say, "It has been good; I have done my best."

THE MEASURE OF AGE

"The measure of age is not the number of years one lives but how well. Some people are old at thirty, while others are young at eighty," so philosophized by neighbor Uncle Orlo.

I had stopped to visit with this good friend, as I often did. He was husking sweet corn there in his garden next to his house. Our subject of conversation was a man known by each of us. This man had reached his ninetieth birthday and was still very much alert in body, mind, and spirit.

Uncle Orlo is gone from this earth, but his philosophy of life and his influence still linger in my mind. He was the kind of man who believed that people grow old by deserting their ideals. He believed that a person was as young as his faith and as old as his doubts, as young as his hope and as old as his despair.

Through the years I have observed my aging friends and have studied my own reflection in the mirror of life. I have concluded that time may bring wrinkles to the skin, but when we lose our enthusiasm and zest for living, we bring wrinkles to our soul.

A wise man of long ago wrote, "The hoary head is a crown of glory, if it be found in the way of righteousness" (Proverbs 16:31). We are not only counseled to grow older gracefully, but the author also observes that gray hair is a "crown of glory" if it is found in a life lived with wisdom and Godlike character.

The land of Canaan was being divided amongst the tribes of Israel as they entered the Promised Land. Caleb, saying that he was eighty-five years of age but still strong, asked not for the easy way but said, "Now therefore give me this mountain..." (Joshua 14:12). At eighty-five years young, he was still climbing mountains.

The number of our years has little to do with our climbing spiritual mountains of faith, wisdom, and courage. As we grow older in years, we learn that there are some mountains in life that are not worth the effort, while others are still a challenge to us. Then we pray for the wisdom to make the right choices.

The measure of one's age depends to a great extent on how well we have invested our lives in the values that are eternal. Jesus once informed His hearers that "The thief cometh not, but for to steal, and to kill, and to destroy: I am come that they might have life, and that they might have it more abundantly" (John 10:10).

The acceptance of the upright life assures us of ageless and eternal living with Him.

"I CAN'T—BUT WE CAN"

Some time ago I was counseling a couple in preparation for their wedding. The prospective groom seemed to be the spokesman of the two. He kept talking about "my" kitchen, "my" wedding picture, and so on. Before the session was over, I concluded that he was troubled with "I" strain with a capital "I."

He was like the man who often boasted, "I have reared six boys for my country." A close friend of the man finally said to him, "Jim, didn't your wife have anything to do with it?"

Recently I had a letter from a follower of one of my columns. She wrote, "I notice that you often speak about "our column." Does someone help you write them?" I answered her letter by saying, "I could not have written, or continue to write, without God's help, my wife's encouragement, and certainly not without those who read and respond to me. Yes, it is 'our column.' "

There are those who believe that you can do anything you want to do if you are sufficiently determined and follow the formula of Paul, the apostle, who tells us: "I can do all things..." (Philippians 4:13). Paul was determined to destroy the Christian movement. He got as far as the road to Damascus. There he was stopped by a power greater than himself.

Yes, you can do anything you want to do if you follow the formula. The Bible is a "We" book. The formula is not "I can" but "We can." It tells of the victories that came to those who trusted not alone in themselves but worked together with God.

Caleb, one of the twelve spies of the Israelites who came back from Canaan, agreed with the majority report that there were giants in the land. But Caleb said, "... Let us go up at once, and possess it; for we are well able to overcome it" (Numbers 13:30).

la does not stop with "I can do all things" but
"through Christ which strengheneth me"
13). I can't, but We can.

Chapter (Hebrews 11) ends by saying, "...that
should not be made perfect." We are a link in
od's plan for the world. No chain is stronger than
k. Those men and women of faith were pioneers,
they began cannot be completed without us.

inority—but God and I are a majority. Many times
alled upon to do something that was more than I
f doing. On those occasions I found myself pray-
I shall fail without You, but with Your help, I
Alone, I could not; with Him, We could ... and
nd We do.

LIFE'S GREATEST POWER—LOVE

vill be remembered for famous accomplishments, but
will be remembered for one achievement above the
ten a great artist is remembered for one famous
e composer for one unusual song.

the apostle, wrote many outstanding letters, but he
ich vein when he wrote the 13th Chapter of I Corin-
this he was at his best as he writes of the greatest
all—Love.

is the lubricant that keeps the machinery of life run-
othly. Love is the element in life that makes two hearts
ne. The presence of love in the home makes it a heaven
; the absence of love can make the home a hell on
incere love helps to minimize the faults of others and
their virtues.

e Bible is filled with many words of wisdom, but the
revelation of all is that of the power of love. Paul,
to the Christians at Corinth, tells them that love does
nk of itself; it has no envy of others; it rejoices in the

truth, and does not think evil. Love never fails in the ti[me] when it is needed most.

Paul ends his warm and urgent chapter by saying, "A[nd] now abideth faith, hope, charity [love], these three; but t[he] greatest of these is charity [love]" (I Corinthians 13:13).

When we think of the power of human live, we disco[ver] that it has no limits. We see the protective love of parents n[ot] only in the human family but in the animal kingdom, and [we] marvel at their willingness to give their lives for their offsprin[g]. Each of us has felt that special, unlimited loyalty of those w[ho] love us.

Victor Hugo, a French poet, wrote, "The greatest happ[i]ness in our life is that we are loved for ourselves, or in spite [of] ourselves." Yes, most of us need more love than we deserve.

The greatest example of love, however, is God's love f[or] us. Once again we hear Paul saying, "But God commendeth H[is] love toward us, in that, while we were yet sinners, Christ die[d] for us" (Romans 5:8). God loves us in spite of ourselves. H[e] loves us not alone for what we are but for what we can become.

Paul, who experienced this forgiving power of God's love entreats the Roman Christians as well as each of us to "Owe n[o] man any thing, but to love one another...." (Romans 13:8).

Although it is essential that we keep faith and hope alive love is the anchor that holds life steady. Love, then, is the greatest power of all. It is love that makes life worth living and peace in eternity certain.

Index

Abel, 54
Abraham, 19, 88, 109
Acceptance, 110
Acts, 36, 103, 129, 135
Afterglow, 66-68
Aging, 30, 161
Aloneness, 150
Ambition, 92
"America" (Smith), 90
Anniversaries, 93-94
Appreciation, 142
Aristotle, 131
Augustine, Saint, 58

Babcock, Maltbie, 141
Balanced rations, 123-24
Beatitudes, 130
Beecher, Henry Ward, 107, 141
Beliefs, sale of, 150-51
Bennett, Arnold, 10
Bixler, Jack, 89
Blessings, counting, 137-51
"Bless This House" (Taylor), 52

Bradford, William, 88
Brock, Blanche, 59
Brock, Fred, 35
Brock, Virgil, 59
Brooks, Phillips, 129, 156, 157
Burning bush, 96
Burroughs, John, 32-33

Cain, 54
Caleb, 22, 78, 115, 161, 162
Carlyle, Thomas, 7
Change, 110
Charity (*see* Love)
Choice, freedom of, 70
Christmas, 152-57
II Chronicles, 143
"Columbus" (Miller), 105
Communication, 131-32
Confusion, 129-30
I Corinthians, 22, 57, 89, 95, 127, 135, 163-64
II Corinthians, 41, 47, 76, 100, 110, 159

Cornell, Will, 45
Courage, 88, 89-90, 102, 105
Criticism, 141
Crosby, Fanny Jane, 38, 39
"Crossing the Bar" (Tennyson), 40

David, 12, 31, 101, 121
Declaration of Independence, 16, 91
Despair, 102, 116-17
Determination, 38-39
Deuteronomy, 76, 88
Discouragement, 99-100
Drugs, 73

Easter, 41-50
Ecclesiastes, 23, 34, 73, 107, 108
Edison, Thomas, 34
Eli, 6
Elijah, 62-63, 113
Elliott, Charlotte, 129
Emerson, Joe, 81-82
Emerson, Ralph Waldo, 20
Encouragement, 57, 126-27
Enoch, 132
Ephesians, 61, 93
Equal rights, 53
Example, power of, 128-29
Excess baggage, 10-11
Exodus, 31, 84
Expectancy, 33-34

Faith, 20, 37-38, 97, 102, 106, 164
Faith Chapter (Hebrews), 19, 54, 83, 163
Family, 52-71
Faulkner, William, 47
Fear, 11, 60-61
Footprints, 54-55
Forgiveness, 97
Fox, George, 103
Franklin, Benjamin, 71, 128

Freedom, 87-91
Friends, 8-9, 132
Frost, Robert, 46
Future, 1-15, 29, 30, 73, 114-15, 117, 160

Galatians, 71, 102, 121
Garfield, James A., 85
Genesis, 10, 61, 132, 148, 150
Gettysburg Address, 17-18
Gideon, 22, 141
Going the second mile, 12-13
Gratitude, 137-39, 141-44, 146-47
Gravity, 5-6
Green, Joan, 97-98
Growing up, 79
Guest, Edgar, 52-53

Habit, 73
Hall, Myrtle, 83
Handicaps, 75-76
Hankey, Katherine, 42
Hannah, 39
Happiness:
    key to, 101-2
    recipe for, 130-31
Harmony, 94-95
Hatred, 10, 22-24, 130
Havergal, Frances, 2
Healing, 55-56
Heatter, Gabriel, 4
Hebrews, 4, 19, 22, 54, 93, 109, 148, 163
Helping ourselves, 122-23
Helplessness, 11-12
Henley, William Ernest, 77
Herford, Oliver, 10
Heritage, 16-28
Hine, Stuart K., 158
Holland, Josiah, 89
Home, 52-71
"Home" (Guest), 52-53

Hope, 38, 102, 104-5, 108-9, 116-17, 157, 164
Hopelessness, 11-12
How Can We Be Truly Happy?, 102
Hugo, Victor, 164
Humility, 143

"If We Understood" (anon), 63, 64
Indifference, 8
Influence, 54
Inspirational experiences, 125-26
Irvin, Jim, 5
Isaiah, 63, 113, 117, 156

Jackson, Andrew, 21
James, 7-8, 32, 115
James, William, 77
Jennings, Glen, 137
Jennings, Margaret Madren, 19
Jennings, Minnie, 45-46, 68, 70, 71, 113, 122, 123, 137
Jennings, Oscar M., 70, 72, 113, 122, 137
Jennings, Samuel, 19
Jennings, Thelma, 13, 69, 70, 93, 94, 109
Jesus, 9, 25, 35, 53, 55, 67, 74, 77-78, 82, 85, 95, 101-2, 106, 113-14, 120, 125, 127, 132, 134, 144, 149, 151, 158, 161
  childhood and young manhood, 66, 79, 103
  Christmas, 153-57
  death of, 22, 40, 43
  healing of, 56, 122-23, 144
  last earthly hours of, 74, 118, 136
  power of example, 128-29
  prayer and, 60, 68, 89, 96, 107, 140, 145
  Resurrection of, 41-50

Sermon on the Mount, 11, 13, 58, 64, 86, 97, 123, 124, 130, 133
  on tomorrow, 30, 115, 160
Job, 83
John, 3, 6, 7, 9, 40, 42, 47-49, 74, 77, 82, 97, 102, 106, 118, 133, 135, 136, 158, 161
I John, 95
Joseph, 10
Joshua, 17, 22, 70, 78, 115, 161
Joy, 74-75, 154
"Joy to the World" (Watts), 155
Judas Iscariot, 25, 151

Keller, Helen, 76
I Kings, 63, 64, 113
Kingsley, Charles, 129
Knepper, Bill, 65

Lauder, Sir Harry, 69
Laughter, 108
Leaven of life, 113-14
Light in the window, 68-69
Lincoln, Abraham, 16, 17-18, 145
Lincoln, Sarah Bush, 16
Lincoln, Thomas, 16
Listening, 62, 63
Lloyd George, David, 135
Loneliness, 149-50
Longfellow, Henry Wadsworth, 54, 92
Looking ahead, 3-4
Lord is my shepherd, The, 31, 92, 121, 145
Love, 11, 22-24, 55-57, 93, 97, 102, 163-64
Love Chapter (I Corinthians), 23, 57
Lowell, James Russell, 6
Lowrey, Robert, 43, 50

167

Luke, 60, 66, 68, 76, 79, 92, 103, 118, 129, 140, 144, 154, 155, 157
Lyte, Henry F., 12

Mark, 35, 46, 49, 55-56, 79, 85, 96, 101
Marriage, 93-94
Marshall, Peter, 48
Martin, Charles D., 92
Mary, 48-49
Mary Magdalene, 48-49, 50
Mason, Tamer, 101
Masterpieces, 65-66
Matthew, 11, 13, 25, 26, 30, 42-45, 48-50, 64, 69, 86, 89, 97, 107, 114, 115, 122-25, 127, 129-31, 134, 139, 145, 150, 151, 155, 160
Mayflower compact, 88
McCreery, John L., 46
McIlwain, Robert, 127
Mercy, 130, 131
Miller, Joaquin, 105
Minority, 22
Moses, 31, 38, 76, 83, 84, 88, 96, 134
Mother's Day, 57, 69
Mountain-top experiences, 125-26

Naomi, 39, 104-5
Napoleon, 8
National Family Week, 57, 69
Needs, 91-92, 123-24, 145
New leaf, 14-15
New opportunities, 1-15
Newton, John, 66, 83, 100
Nicodemus, 158
Noah, 22, 148
Nostalgia, 159
Numbers, 162

Obedience, 103-4
Orpah, 39

Paderewski, Ignace, 85
Past, 1-3, 29, 72, 114-15, 159-60
Patience, 7-8, 32-33, 56
Paul, 33, 36, 47, 53, 57, 61, 68, 74, 76, 89, 90, 93, 95, 100, 102, 103, 110, 111, 116, 119, 121, 127, 135, 140, 146, 147, 159, 162, 163-64
Peace, 4, 96-98, 117-18, 153, 157, 164
"Peace, Peace, Wonderful Peace" (Cornell), 45
Perfection, 85-86
Peter, 7, 15, 25, 26, 83, 120, 125, 26, 129, 135
II Peter, 7
Philippians, 33, 111, 119, 146, 147, 162, 163
Poole, William C., 41
Potential, 34-35
Power, 62-63, 112-13
Praise, 141
Prayer, 60, 68, 89, 96, 102, 107, 139-40, 145
Prejudice, 10
Prodigal Son, 92, 146
Proverbs, 2, 4, 73, 115, 119, 121, 122, 141, 150, 161
Psalms, 2, 3, 8, 12, 18, 26-28, 30, 31, 37, 58, 59, 61, 62, 71, 80, 91, 92, 95, 101, 112, 116, 121, 129, 138, 139, 144, 145, 147, 160
Puritans, 87-88, 139, 142-43

Rainbow, 147-48
Relaxation, 95-96
Resting, 101

Resurrection, 41-50
Revelation, 3, 23
Revenge, 130, 131
Rogers, Will, 27
Romans, 57, 116, 140, 164
Roosevelt, Franklin D., 96-97
Roots, 16-17, 19
Ruskin, John, 32
Ruth, 39, 104-5
Ruth, Babe, 34

Sammis, John, 103-4
Samson, 75
Samuel, 6, 39
I Samuel, 6-7
Sandburg, Carl, 17, 55
Selflessness, 130, 131
Sermon on the Mount, 11, 13, 58, 64, 86, 97, 123, 124, 130, 133
Shakespeare, William, 133
Shaw, Matthew J., 126
Silas, 36
Singing, 59-60
Smiling, 59-60, 108
Smith, Margaret Chase, 129
Smith, Samuel F., 90
Solitude, 149-50
Solomon, 64, 143
Songs at midnight, 35-36
Spafford, Horatio, 100
Speaking acquaintance, 131, 132
Speech, freedom of, 21
Sunday, Billy, 47

Taylor, Helen, 52
Television commercials, 6
Ten Commandments, 133
Tennyson, Alfred, 1, 40
Thanksgiving, 138-39, 142-44

I Thessalonians, 68, 74, 140
Thinking, 118-19
Time to Remember, A (Jennings), 24, 25, 159
Timothy, 74
II Timothy, 53, 74
Touching, 55-56
Trust, 7, 118, 119
Trying, 118, 119
Twain, Mark, 108

Ulmer, L. F., 141-42
Understanding, 63-65
Unity, 94-95

Values, 27-28
Van Dyke, Henry, 57
Victorious living, 110-11, 118-19
Vigilance, 89
Vision, 87, 88

Wants, 91-92, 145
War, 17-18, 24-25
Warren, John, 90
Washington, George, 70, 142
Watts, Isaac, 12, 155
Weeping, 107-8
Wells, Amos R., 39
Wesley, John, 85
White, Norma, 8
Wihtol, Austris, 132
Wilberforce, Ernest R., 160
Winners, mark of, 82-83
Worries, 29-30
Worship, freedom of, 21

Youth, 72-73

Zacchaeus, 76
Zechariah, 12